VOICES *of*
LEIGH-ON-SEA

JUDITH WILLIAMS

VOICES *of*
LEIGH-ON-SEA

JUDITH WILLIAMS

The
History
Press

First published 2012

The History Press
The Mill, Brimscombe Port
Stroud, Gloucestershire, GL5 2QG
www.thehistorypress.co.uk

British Library Cataloguing in Publication Data.
A catalogue record for this book is available from the British Library.

ISBN 978 0 7524 5938 7

Typesetting and origination by The History Press
Printed in Great Britain

CONTENTS

ACKNOWLEDGEMENTS

I would like to thank everyone who has assisted me with finding contacts, supplying photographs and general support, in particular: Steve Aylen, Pat Pollard, Christine Selby, Peter Thorn, Kathryn Ash, Maggie Briley, Barrie Adcock, Carole Mulroney, Janice Matthews, Janet Young, Kiti Theobald, Roger Rolph, Warwick Conway, Rob King, Kathy Harvey, Ian Hawks, Lianne Burtonshaw, Nicki Little, Jane Plummer, Kate Herbert, Leslie Head, www. FootstepsPhotos.co.uk, and the staff of Priory House and Priory Day Centre.

But, of course, this book would never have seen the light of day without the 'stars', my wonderful interviewees, who were all so kind and generous. I'm sorry I didn't have room for everything. Thank you so much for your help; I loved meeting you all: Pat Bailey (*née* Humphress), Vivienne Barker (*née* Rush), Harry Bayford, Geoffrey Brown, Malcolm Buckler, Marian Cove, Keith Cox, Norman Crane, Heather Curry (*née* Skinner), Val Dack (*née* Mowbray), Averil Eve (*née* Evans), Terry Fane, David Flack, Donald Fraser, Ruby Frost (*née* Loveland), Mike Grimwade, Jean Hamilton (*née* Fisher), Joan Herbert (*née* Cole), Renee Horner (*née* Palmer), Phyllis Jackson (*née* Plumb), Wyn Johnson (*née* Turner), Ellen King, Archie Kirby, Denis Kirby, Dorothy Lewis (*née* Nightingale), David Little, Janice Matthews (*née* Barker), Tom Mayhew, Wendy Newby (*née* Treble), Thelma Nicol (*née* Sawyer), Arthur Perkins, Joy Perkins (*née* Attwood), Freda Plimmer, Albert Plummer, Pearl Plummer (*née* Pierce), Irene Reynolds, Derek Rowe, Shirley Rowe (*née* Clark), Bernard Sadler, Connie Satchwell, Christine Selby (*née* Blower), Sylva Sheffield (*née* Walling), Betty Smith (*née* Murray), Winifred Stone, Don Stoneman, Annette Tidman (*née* Luck), John Tyler, Ray Warman, Doris Williams (*née* Rowley), Geoffrey Williams, Richard Woodley, Kathleen Young (*née* Kidd), Michael Young.

One

EARLY MEMORIES

Suet Puddings, Toast and Dripping

I was born in Queens Road in 1919. It was very steep walking home down the unbuilt corner of Redcliff Drive, but I loved to run down it – one of the simple joys of life. I also remember coming down Church Hill on roller skates, but that was not as thrilling as I thought it would be and I was scared stiff!

Where Grand Court flats are now was a miniature golf course. There were also wooden slot machines which you put your penny in and it went round and round; if it went all the way to the bottom you got your penny back but, invariably, it went down the hole in the middle and you lost your penny.

On Sundays Mother took me to Christ Church, the Reformed Episcopal Church of England in Pall Mall, dressed up in my Sunday best: white lace gloves and always a hat.

I was brought up on suet puddings and toast with dripping on but, whatever we ate, I was never allowed to talk at the table, or put my elbows on it.

In the school holidays, Mother would pack up some sandwiches and a glass bottle of lemonade and I'd take my brother Eric, three years younger than me, out for the day. We'd go down to the cliffs and the beach. We loved to stand on the Gypsy Bridge and get enveloped in steam when a train went underneath. We thought that was marvellous! We also liked to stand on the iron gates when they opened up on the level crossing by The Ship. If the signalman didn't see us, we got a ride round while the gates opened. We learnt to swim at the open air swimming pool along the front but they closed it down, saying it was unhealthy.

Ruby Frost

Racing Carts

When we moved to Edinburgh Avenue in 1926, our garden was deep with ruts and I thought, 'I don't think much of this!' I got all covered in mud. However, Mother and Dad soon had it laid out with a rose garden, a lawn and a willow tree, which I sat under in the hot summers.

The greengrocer brought his horse and cart round to the door but the butcher would come round to take orders, and the grocer's boy came for orders once a week. Your goods would be sent round later that day. Mum got fed up with them keep coming round!

For a long time there were only two cars in our road and they were decrepit: kept together with string! Therefore, the road was our playground. We had long skipping ropes and did lots of skipping, tying one end to a lamp post and stretching the rope along the road. We had races from the top to the bottom of our road, and once had carts for racing down the road. I think my mum made mine for me. There was enough room in it for me and my friend Mary Hopkins.

Kathleen Young

Sliding Down the Cockles

On Sundays in the '20s, we liked to go and slide down the heaps of cockle shells behind the cockle sheds. Our white Sunday clothes would end up black! My mother had a copper out in the shed but she never used it. She brought the bath indoors and put it on the gas, and tipped in three or four saucepans of water for doing the washing.

I loved the cinema when I was a girl. The Corona, the Empire and the Coliseum: I went to them all. Children were half-price. After the film, I'd go out to the toilet and then go in [to the cinema] again when they all started coming in and the film came on again. My mother had to come and drag me out.

Pearl Plummer

Olive Mann (later Olive Tyler), far left, and friends dancing in the Empire Palace, *c.* 1910. (John Tyler)

Winkles for Tea

Mum did the washing in a big copper on the gas stove in the scullery and then put it through the mangle in the back garden. Water for our baths, too, would have to be heated in a tub on the gas rings. The bath itself hung in the shed and it would be brought into the scullery once a week.

Kenny Dolby lived near us in Leighville Grove and came round selling fish, cockles and winkles from a barrow. It was the cheapest way to buy them. On Sunday afternoons, the family would go for a walk along past Leigh station to Hadleigh. Then we'd come home and have winkles for tea with bread and butter.

David Flack

'On the Flicker'

In the 1930s we were living in Surrey Avenue. Southend Council had a system to keep your electricity bills down – you had your lights 'on the flicker', with a special meter that limited the number of watts you could switch on. For example, if you went upstairs, you had to switch the kitchen light off otherwise they all flickered on and off. My old man lost his temper with the meter one day and bashed the living daylights out of it and all the lights came on.

In 1946, when I came home from the RAF, I bought my mum an electric iron for Christmas (to replace one you heated up over the gas). I went upstairs to try it out, plugged the iron in, switched it on and all the lights went berserk! Soon after that they stopped the flicker system.

We always went to my nan's in Sunningdale Avenue for Christmas. Auntie Gert did all the cooking, Christmas puddings and lovely homemade marmalade – I can taste it now. I thought Christmas lasted two weeks because Mum took me and my brother round there several days before Christmas and we stayed for several days afterwards. Uncle Arthur, Auntie Alice, cousins Arthur and Gladys came down from London for Christmas but had to leave on Boxing Day evening to get on the train to get back for work the next day, and I thought 'How dreadful!' We had some lovely Christmases.

Denis Kirby

A Strict Vicar

We moved to Henry Drive in 1937 when I was seven years old and I enjoyed going down to Belfairs Woods to join the boys and girls jumping over ditches.

The Walker brothers built all the roads around our way. Mr Walker lived on the corner of Tennyson Close with his grandmother, and often came round to see us. He kept a yacht at Paglesham and he'd take us out for trips on the Crouch.

Our doctor was on the corner of Walker Drive and the London Road. He was an Irishman and a very strict Catholic. We'd see his wife pushing the baby in the pram and two little ones holding on either side, while the doctor himself would walk along twirling his walking stick.

Sundays meant going to St Margaret's Church for service in the morning and Sunday school

Children's Christmas party at Christ Church, Pall Mall, early 1930s. (John Tyler)

in the afternoon. The vicar was the very strict Father Head and the incense made me feel sick. I used to have to go out of the service until I felt better.

For church we wore our navy blue reefer coats and our school hats: panama in the summer, velour in the winter and berets in the rain. My sister once threw my hat over a garden wall. I was terrified to go in to get it back.

You had to go halfway across the road to get on the trams on the London Road and [had to] hope a car wasn't coming!

Ellen King

A Nasty Accident

I was born in Leigham Court Drive in June 1919, but we soon moved to Southsea Avenue. There were no steps on Church Hill then and we used to be able to roller skate all the way down.

We paid our rates at the police station in Elm Road. The library was in that same building until the new library opened in Broadway West, and it was also where you took new babies to be registered.

In 1927, I was once playing with my friend in Rectory Grove when I fell over some of the uneven paving stones that were being laid in preparation for making Broadway West and I hurt my arm. I screamed so much that Mum heard it from our living room in Southsea Avenue and rushed up to see what had happened. Two old dears on their way to the new library, just opened in Broadway West, called out to me, 'Stop making that noise!' They didn't know how much pain I was in!

Mum laid me on the bed in our front room (set up because she did a bit of letting in the summer months) and called the doctor. He said my arm was broken and I needed an ambulance to take me to hospital. However, it cost 10s for an ambulance and we couldn't afford that. So, we walked up to The Broadway to get the tram and Dad spoke to the driver and asked him not to pull up with any jerks. We took the tram to Victoria Circus and walked down to the Victoria Hospital in Warrior Square. The doctor in charge said, 'She'll have to lose that arm, come back tomorrow.' He strapped my arm to my body and we took the tram back home.

The next day we travelled to Southend again – 2d for my mum and 1d for my fare. At the hospital they said they couldn't see me until four o'clock, so we had to walk around Southend until then, and find ourselves some food.

When I was finally admitted to the hospital, the doctor decided he could save my arm, which had a compound fracture. I was in hospital for two or three weeks on one of the two children's wards. Although it was November, we had some lovely weather and some patients were taken outside in their beds.

When I came home, my mother had to massage my arm every night and pull it, so it healed right. My brothers loved it: 'Let me have a pull now!' I had to go to the hospital three times a week for exercises and it took about two years to heal properly.

I couldn't play the piano again until then, but I did go back and learn but I didn't like going every week. Mum said, 'Alright, have your own way, but you will regret it.' … and I do.

Wyn Johnson

Wyn Johnson with her mother and brother, Bert, at the clinic in Leigh council offices in Elm Road (now the police station), 1919. (Wyn Johnson *née* Turner)

May Fair in the Rectory Gardens, 1920s. Norman Crane once won a coconut for an old lady who was born in 1835, and Joy Perkins remembers, 'The trees were gay with flags and fairy lights. I once tried the aerial flight, hanging on to a pulley which slid down a wire.'

Fancy Dress

Around 1925, I met Peggy Mount at a party at St Clement's Church hall, given by my music mistress, Mrs Grey. We had to wear fancy dress and I had a gnome costume with a hood, which I had worn before at a school event. Soon after I arrived at the party, the adults introduced me to an elf and thought we looked sweet together, so we held hands and went around together for the rest of the afternoon. When it came time to say goodbye, the elf and I took off our hoods and found out that we were both little boys. Our five-year-old manhood was mortified!

I had a similar experience in later life, aged fourteen, when I dressed up as a girl with a flower in my hair to take part in the Southend Carnival. I walked all the way to Southend with my friend and collected 4s 10½d. Someone grabbed me and tried to kiss me! Then I lost my friend in the crowd and had to walk home alone. But at least I raised 4s 10½d for the hospital.

Norman Crane

Fog Horns

In the '50s I lived in Manchester Drive and on any foggy day you could distinctly hear the fog horns of ships in the estuary. There was usually a line of cargo ships at any time because London docks and Tilbury were in full operation. We could also hear the barking 'chuff, chuff' of steam trains pulling out of Chalkwell station. There were numerous foggy days in the '50s

Derek Rowe and his sister Vera in the Southend Carnival, *c.* 1929. (Derek Rowe)

and occasional smog.

The entire field where Darlinghurst School now stands was allotments – by my day mostly abandoned. It was our customary play area.

Don Stoneman

Games

A game I enjoyed with my brothers and sisters was 'bad eggs': one person was 'out' and would throw a ball up in the air while calling out one of a given list of items. Whoever had chosen the particular thing that was called out had to chase the ball while everyone else ran. Then the idea was to bowl the ball to hit the legs of anyone that they could reach.

In Olive Avenue, we played hopscotch with stones. The pattern of the paving stones was perfect. We started with a single paving stone in the middle as number one, and then two and three were written in chalk on the double above, numbering to twelve. The idea was to hop,

Birthday party, 1950s. Standing: Janet Carroll, ?, Elizabeth Potterton. Sitting: Vivien Thomas, Dorothy Nightingale, Averil Evans, Stephanie Allen, Helena Vacuic. Averil says, 'Near the bus stop between Thames Drive and Cottesmore Gardens was a patch of wasteland. On Guy Fawkes night, the locals would take their Golden Rain, sparklers, rockets, etc. and set them off so that all could share in the delights. Looking back, it was positively dangerous!' (Averil Eve *née* Evans)

jump, stand on a leg on the numbers in turn to pick up the stone. The winner was the one who collected a stone from each number and returned to base with it before throwing it again, until all twelve had been successfully targeted.

We played 'he' on the cliffs below Marine Parade and were allowed to climb trees to get away from the person chosen to be 'he'.

Averil Eve

Belfairs

Before the war, there was an airbase where Belfairs School is now and Mum used to take me to watch the planes take off. They held shows and exhibitions there every so often.

Betty Smith

Romanies and Farmworkers

My Great Aunt Lou and Great Uncle Jack lived off Green Lane in the '20s, where they used to grow a lot of stuff and sell it. Lou had a well in her front garden but no running water. To visit them from Southend, we caught the bus to the Woodcutters' and from there had to walk down Bellhouse Lane and up to Green Lane. Aunt Lou's daughters would take me to pick flowers, sloes and wild plums. They caught rabbits in the woods and hedgehogs for eating. They'd roll the hedgehogs in clay and pull all the prickles off. I think they said it tasted like chicken. There was very few people about in that area – only some Romanies and farmworkers.

Belfairs Woods came up over where Woodside is now, and then there was meadowland and fields down towards the A127. Everything grew in the woods: bluebells, cowslips, primroses, the lot. When they built the bungalows that are there now, they ruined it.

A lot of gypsy families came to the Woodcutters Avenue area in their caravans for the winter. They'd go over to Kent in the summer for the hop picking, and to Cambridge for fruit picking. A lot of them never bothered to get married, so old Father Rice came up and married them all for nothing.

When I first moved to Mountain Ash Avenue in the '60s, there was nothing north of it. From there I could see the trains coming from Rochford as they travelled to Hockley and on to Rayleigh. They were steam trains, so you could hear them too. My friend who lived at the top of Eastwood Rise near Gravel Road said that before the war they could see the postman walking from the Elms pub at Leigh – that's how open it was.

Winifred Stone

Woodcutters' Arms, Eastwood Road North, 1920s. To get to Green Lane from Southend, Winifred Stone had to get off the bus here and walk the rest of the way.

Played in the Fields

My earliest memories are of when my family lived in a bungalow at the bottom of Crescent Road, which ran downhill from London Road to Western Road. At that time there were no houses beyond our road and we played in the fields.

Whilst we were living there, when I was about five years old, the R101 airship went slowly over our house, from the south, travelling northwards. I was ill in bed with chicken pox at the time and my mother ordered me back to bed because I was leaning out of the window, watching it go over.

Thelma Nicol

Pneumonia

In 1927 I became very ill. My mother's sister, only nine years older than me and about thirteen at the time, took me out tobogganing, after which I found myself partially paralysed. The doctor was called. He thought I had meningitis and promptly walked out again as there was no treatment at the time. I was put to bed, but when our usual doctor called he pronounced I had bronchial pneumonia. The treatment at the time was poulticing on the back and chest. I came through the crisis and the doctor regarded it as a miracle, putting my recovery down to my stamina and the heat. My relations were all downstairs praying for me, I'm told.

Mother was grateful to the doctor for saving my life, but his bill came to £300 in those days before the NHS, and we took lodgers for some time to help get the debt paid off. Quite how much this sum amounted to in terms of our income I am not sure, but I do know that a few years later, in 1932, my father was earning the very respectable sum of £3 per week.

Phyllis Jackson

Stair Rods Polished

Our three-storey family house at 101 Hadleigh Road, where I lived from 1914 until I married in 1938, had two large reception rooms, a large kitchen with a scullery off [it] and a small lounge hall. Upstairs were four bedrooms, a bathroom and toilet on the first floor, and a large attic bedroom that went over the whole of the house on the second floor. Mother and Dad had modern fireplaces fitted and some blocked up, a new 'marlexa' bathroom and a washbasin in my room.

Mother always had a maid to live-in to do the housework and breakfasts but cooked the main meal herself. A girl came each day to take me for a walk and a woman came in once a week to do the mending. Dad was not a rich man but help was cheaper and easier to get, so it was quite usual to have help if you could afford it. Dad also had a gardener once a week. Housework was not so easy in those days with no electric cleaners or washing machines; even irons had to be heated up on the stove. The front and back steps had to be whitened each day, brass stair rods polished, and once a week tea leaves were squeezed out and spread on the carpet to lay the dust, then the carpet was brushed with a hard broom.

Essex Yacht Club children's party in St Clement's Church hall, 1936. Shirley Rowe is in the centre of the back row as an Eastern princess; her brother, Martyn, is an Eastern prince, fifth from right in the second row. (Shirley Rowe *née* Clark)

One very cold winter in the 1920s, our pipes froze and Dad, in trying to thaw them out in the roof, burst the pipe and, jumping back, put his foot through the ceiling. Fortunately, it happened to be over the bath but the floor of the bathroom got flooded and the water seeped through into the hall below. Lots of people had similar trouble and a man from the Water Company came each day to open up a stopcock in Hadleigh Road, where people queued with kettles, saucepans and pails to get their water for the day.

On the corner of the road was an old-fashioned lamp post with a little door in the bottom that could be opened, and my friend Laurie Street thought this was our private hiding place for little notes or acorns, etc.

Joy Perkins

Disappearing Balloon

We moved to Elmsleigh Drive in 1933 when I was ten months old. An early recollection is of sitting on a red balloon amongst a lot of legs, the bodies of which occupied all the seats. A sudden bang so startled me that I failed to notice how my balloon had managed to disappear. I never did find it.

Grandma and Grandad often came from Dagenham for Sunday tea, and we would walk along the cinderpath to wave at the train and then run up to the entrance of Leigh station to meet them.

During this time we enjoyed picnics in Belfairs Woods, paddling on the seafront and feeding the gulls along the cinderpath. When I was four, Dad bought a small car, a Morris 8, so we had outings to look forward to.

Doris Williams

Uncle Toot

My dad had been a sergeant major in the Royal Engineers and his commanding officer was squire of a village in Suffolk and also managing director of Tootal Ties. He would drive down to Southend in his Humber car and stop outside our shop and toot his horn. We called him Uncle Toot.

'I can't abide hotels, I'll stay with you,' he'd say when he arrived unexpectedly. We all had to share a bed, so he could have a bed to himself. We used to have porridge and tea for breakfast but Mum cooked a fried breakfast with eggs, bacon and grapefruit for Uncle Toot, which made us drool. Once, he didn't even eat the breakfast; he let it go cold and stubbed his big cigar out in it. Then he threw two big white fivers on the table and said, 'There's some pocket money for the children' and off he went. We'd never seen so much money! We rinsed off the breakfast and ate it, while Mum used one of the fivers to get her wedding ring out of the pawnshop.

Tom Mayhew

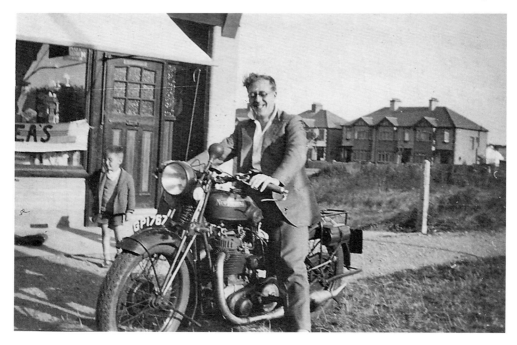

Little Tom Mayhew and a family friend visiting the shop at Kent Elms Corner, 1933. The field in the background is now the site of Essex Ford. (Tom Mayhew)

Sunday Best

I was born in North Street in 1943. We lived in the upstairs with my nan, and my aunt and her family lived downstairs. The bath was a tin tub, kept outside, and we had to go down through my aunt's house to get to the outside toilet. Mum had a big boiler in the kitchen, a butler sink and a mangle outside the back door. In the garden we kept Nelly, a chicken. I don't know if we were supposed to eat her, but we never did.

When the milkman came past, everyone ran out with buckets and spades to get the manure his horse left behind.

Nan made a lot of our clothes; she was always knitting and sewing. I had loads of knitted boleros in all different colours of angora wool. However, when we went to Sunday school in the chapel in Station Road, we had to wear our Sunday best, which was stripped off us the minute we got home. After Sunday school we often walked down to the cockle sheds to buy our cockles and shrimps for Sunday tea. I liked the brown shrimps, which you bought in a net bag. Back home, it was the children's job to use a pin to take the black bits off the winkles and take them out of their shells. We ended up with the black bits stuck all over our faces. I didn't like winkles, but the adults ate them with vinegar and pepper.

Pat Bailey

Soaked in Vinegar

Sundays in the '50s meant Sunday school at Belfairs Methodist Church, dressed to the hilt with hat, coat and gloves to match. I even took part in a Sunday school play there, dressed up as a little African girl, black face and all, as we had recently returned from living in East Africa.

On Sunday afternoons, we often visited Belfairs Park for afternoon teas, with horse rides around the park. My parents were frequent visitors to Mummery's Garden Centre in Eastwood Road North, and filled our front garden with red, white and blue flowers.

The rag-and-bone man would come round with his horse and cart, and the coalman delivered sacks of coal through the house. A horse and cart also delivered vegetables.

I attended the local Brownies, walking home unaccompanied in the dark evenings and eating chips. By the time I got home, my gloves were soaked in vinegar.

Heather Curry

Wash Day

Monday was washing day, which meant that we had boiled cod with rice pudding for lunch. You had to keep filling up the copper with jugs of water and then empty it with jugs again. When it was full, it was far too heavy to lift up. There was an airer in the kitchen with five rows to hang the washing on, so we couldn't have a table in the kitchen, or the washing would have dripped on it.

We had a back boiler behind the fireplace so, even in the summer, if you wanted hot water for a bath, you had to have the fire alight.

Pat Bailey enjoying an al fresco bath in North Street, *c.* 1944. (Pat Bailey *née* Humphress)

Outside in the shed we had a mangle, and we would do the mangling out there, with the water running down into a big tub.

John Tyler

Stuck in the Grills

I remember Mum taking me up Canvey Road in the '30s to the London Road to see the Duchess of York (later the Queen Mother) come by on her way to open the new Southend Hospital.

Another early memory is of looking out of my bedroom window towards the tennis courts up towards the London Road and getting my head stuck in the grills that we had on the window.

My father was a sidesman at St Clement's when Canon King was the rector. He was a lovely looking man with white hair; we'd see him striding around the town in his robes.

I remember going on a houseboat where they sold sweets and tea, but I've only ever had one cockle and I chewed that for about half an hour – it was like eating a piece of India rubber! We often had winkles for tea.

Before the war we did quite a bit of hoop bowling, and roller skating at the rink in Pavilion Drive. In the snow we had a wooden toboggan with a box on the back for dry gloves, and we used to go down the cliffs at Leigh towards Belton Way – I can see Mum's kitchen now with all

Pat Bailey (far left) as a snowflake at a North Street School concert, *c.* 1949. (Pat Bailey *née* Humphress)

our wet things hanging round it. We'd have a coffee or a hot drink, a change of clothes and then off we'd go back out again for another go.

Shirley Rowe

Boy Scouting

In about 1934/35, when I was nine years old, I went to see my first show at the Empire Palace cinema. It was *Emile and the Detectives* and was a great treat.

I went to Cubs at Wesley Methodist church about that same time. We did a lot of outdoor activities and camping but never had to worry about getting our parents' permission. Mrs Kittridge was the Akela and Tom Parrinder, a lovely man, was the Scoutmaster. Tom spent a lifetime in Scouting and was very well-respected.

Donald Fraser

Guesthouse Assistant

After the war, my gran and grandad had a guesthouse on the corner of Leighcliff Road and Grand Parade. From when I was about ten years old, I'd get the bus straight from Bournemouth Park Road School to Leigh on Fridays to help out over the weekend.

Grand Parade, looking towards Highcliff Drive, *c.* 1930.

The large guesthouse was very busy, sometimes having twenty to thirty guests at a time. They would pay about £3 per week, for which they would get three hot meals a day, plus morning and afternoon tea. One guest paid less as she buttered all the bread for everyone. Gran did work hard, doing all the cooking herself in a little cubby hole in the kitchen, but her food was first class. She never skimped. It was served up in a big dining room with a massive table for all the guests. Grandad would do a lot of the shopping: fish from the Leigh Road and rabbits from Mr Hare, the butcher in the Talza Arcade at Southend. I would take the guests up their tea in the morning, for which they would give me sixpence tip. Some of the guests were full-time, like Mr Wiseman who commuted up to London every day and Mrs Heathman.

There was no heating, of course, and only one bathroom and one toilet. One day, Mrs Heathman wanted a bath, so Gran put a bit of fat on the fire to hurry it up a bit. Then she took me up to The Grand. When we came back, the firemen were outside the house and the chimney was on fire! She had to pay a fine for that, but Mrs Heathman said, 'My bath was lovely and hot!'

Gran was a tiny little woman who didn't eat a lot but she did love her Guinness. If she ran out, I'd go up to the Grand Hotel and get some more for her. That was when I was just ten years old … and they'd serve me! Gran also had a regular order of twenty-four bottles delivered from the Woodfield Road off-licence and said it kept her going. She might have been right – she lived to over ninety.

If the guesthouse was full, Gran would send people to another guesthouse, round the corner. On those days, I had to give up my bed and sleep on a little bed behind a curtain in the hall. There was another guesthouse, further along towards Chalkwell, where the Dagenham Girl Pipers stayed. I'd stand outside and listen to them practising.

The reception for the wedding of Mary Stanbridge to Robert Campbell Dick at the Grand Hotel, 1910. Then only eleven years old, it was a very popular and prestigious venue. (Kiti Theobald)

My mum would come up on the bus on a Sunday with a huge bunch of gladioli that she grew herself, clean clothes for me and all the guesthouse linen: tablecloths, napkins, sheets and bedding that she had washed.

In the afternoons, Gran would have a sleep. If my brother was with me, we'd roll down the cliffs to the seafront and find someone down there to play with.

I'd stay at the guesthouse until Monday morning when I would get the bus from opposite the Corona cinema in the Leigh Road, change at Victoria Circus, and go straight to school. I'd have all the tips in my pocket and, one day, a girl reported me and I had to go to the headmaster and explain where I'd got all that money from. When I got home, I'd give the money to my mum.

Val Dack

'As Good as Gold'

My grandmother's association with Leigh began around 1911 when she and her husband, Vincent Young, set up a theatre company and put on an annual pantomime in Leigh.

By the Second World War, Grandmother Hilda was living in a flat above a chiropodist at Oriel House, 2 Rectory Grove, and I stayed with her there on several occasions during the

The Grand Hotel, *c.* 1900. Marian Cove says, 'In the '50s, it was very, very nice with four bars and a lovely ballroom upstairs.'

Hilda Young *née* Sharpe, who ran a theatre group in Leigh, *c.* 1912. (Malcolm Buckler)

1950s. Trips from London on the steam train were the highlight of the year and I couldn't wait to run down to the Old Town for a plate of cockles. The Old Town was packed in those days with so many competitive sheds boiling up the shellfish, and a huge pile of shells mounting up behind.

I was only about five years old but I recall Grandmother's building was simple, with rendered external walls dashed with small, round pea-gravel. As a treat, I was allowed to climb out of the sitting room window and onto the flat roof which overlooked the street, where my most enjoyable pastime was pulling the round pebbles and little shells out of the pebbledash. 'Malcolm is as good as gold when he is on the roof, so quiet!' I also remember the wonderful sound of the church bells from that privileged vantage point.

By then Grandmother had horrendous arthritis in her fingers but I recently found out that, before she was married, she had been a talented singer, actress and musician, who had toured the British Isles with a music hall company, later giving piano lessons to support her family. To me, however, Grandmother was just a dear old lady who showed me how to boil an egg in her austere little flat in Leigh, while I was in charge of the egg timer.

Malcolm Buckler

Two

SCHOOL DAYS

Starting at West Leigh

On my first day at West Leigh in 1928, I was taken into a class where the teacher wore her hair in the style of 'earphones' – the fashion at the time. We had little wooden chairs and desks, and a slate and chalk each, together with an eraser made of a pad of soft material like carpet underlay, tied round the middle with a wide red paper band. Round the walls were a pictorial alphabet and coloured discs, pasted in patterns of numbers up to twelve.

Miss Bradbury's class: Standard 3, West Leigh School, 1932. The class is under the supervision of supply teacher Miss Appleby, who is standing on the left at the back. (Phyllis Jackson *née* Plumb)

At the end of each day we had to stack our chairs on the desks and stand by them, waiting for the words of dismissal. Occasionally, to quieten us down, we got the command 'hands on heads', when we linked our fingers and sat silent for several minutes.

There was a cloakroom where we each had our own named peg but the lavatories were outdoors. In the concrete playground was a drinking fountain, with a metal cup on a chain.

The house system was St Andrew (blue), St Patrick (green), St David (yellow) and St George (red).

Phyllis Jackson

Empire Day

I was very happy at West Leigh School, although my teacher was a friend of my mother and insisted on calling me 'Normie', which was embarrassing. We had Empire Day celebrations in the presence of the Mayor and Mayoress, when we dressed up as Australian fruit growers, Canadian cowboys or even very politically incorrect Red Indians, and strutted about declaiming our superiority to the rest of the world – at eight years old! How simple we were!

Norman Crane

St George's, Hadleigh Road, 1920s

I started school at St George's, Hadleigh Road, in 1920 and enjoyed maths, art, geography and literature.

Empire Day at West Leigh, 1930s. (Derek Rowe)

The school itself was a large house, built on the hill. The dining room, the staff room and the headmistresses' study were in the house. There were two small cloakrooms under the main house and two small classrooms for the younger children on the same level. There was a courtyard and garden at the back of the house where pupils played hopscotch and 'he' at break time. A large greenhouse was turned into another classroom during my stay at school. Beyond this was The Hut, a large wooden building in the school grounds, reached in the winter by a covered walkway we called the Monks' Passage. The Hut was divided into four classrooms by curtains, with a fifth on the platform where the senior class sat. It had a corrugated roof and was heated by a stove with big black pipes running down the length of the walls. It had two large barn-type doors opening out to the grounds, overlooking the tennis court, orchard and Old Leigh beyond.

All the school took drill classes, marching, arm swinging, etc, and a gymnastic display was held in The Hut just before Christmas.

In the summer, as we only had one tennis court, we did not get much opportunity to play as it was mostly reserved for the senior school team. The rest of us had to play 'pat ball' at the bottom of the orchards. This was on a board which had been erected the height of a tennis net, the idea being to see how many times we could hit the ball onto the wood. However, whilst we were supposed to play 'pat ball', we used to roam about and pick wild strawberries and talk to an old goat named Adolphus.

Empire Day at West Leigh, 1930. Leslie Head says, 'I certainly do not remember dancing round the May Pole or anything like that. Heaven forbid! But I do remember getting a medal to commemorate the Silver Jubilee of King George V in 1935, and another medal for the Coronation of King George VI.' (Joan Herbert *née* Cole)

Empire Day at West Leigh, 1930s. The infant school reception classes are now on this site.
(Phyllis Jackson née Plumb)

To watch hockey matches, we had to walk the length of Marine Parade, which in those days (1920s) finished at Canvey Road, then cross two muddy fields to the school field somewhere near where Tattersall Gardens is now. When this land was built on, we moved to a field where Belfairs School now is.

Annual sports day was fun and I usually ran in the house relay team and the 100 yards. We'd run off the heats for long jump on the beach before morning school.

At the end of the summer term we lined up alphabetically throughout the senior school and filed in for our end-of-year exams. Then, in the afternoon, we rehearsed for the end-of-year play and prize-giving, which was held in St Clement's Hall in Rectory Grove.

St George's evacuated to Dunstable at the beginning of the war and the headmistresses, Miss Axford and Miss Middleton, stayed on in their retirement.

Joy Perkins

They Didn't Like Us

I went to North Street School until I was eleven. Then I went to West Leigh. There were about five of us from the Old Town started at West Leigh at the same time, but they didn't like us; a lot of people thought the Old Town was slums.

Renee Horner

Miss Durrant and Miss Cobley at West Leigh School, 1930s. (Derek Rowe)

A Dragon of a Teacher

I started West Leigh School in 1930 but after a few weeks went down with chicken pox, was very ill with inflamed tonsils and was taken to a nursing home in Chalkwell.

When I went back to school the next September it was to a dragon of a teacher, which didn't help me at all. She made some children stand at the front of the class while she made fun of them. Having missed so much school, I was struggling. However, I then went up into the girls' class for a year and had a nice teacher. Then we were reorganised into the junior school. The headmaster was Mr Gibbs, who I thought was rather pompous – I didn't like him. He would assemble the whole school in the playground and tell us how bad we were.

My father found my maths homework difficult and got himself in such a state about it, because he couldn't do it. My mother asked if I could go and study at my friend Winnie Herbert's house in Bailey Road. I studied for the scholarship in my last year and was surprised to get through, going up to Westcliff High School for Girls in 1936.

Kathleen Young

A Fearsome Headteacher

The first teacher I had at West Leigh when I was five was a Miss Steel. Mr Gibbs was the headmaster. He was a nice man and a very good head, although I thought he was quite fearsome at the time. While I was there they built an extension down by the London Road and we had orders to keep it nice. My journey to school took us straight down Bailey Road and then straight on across the cornfield at the end, where the Scout hut is now. That would bring us out to the Eastwood Road.

I always came home for lunch, walking along the fields along the north side of the London Road. There was a big pond on the corner by Eastwood Road, which I once fell in. I knew my mother would have been furious, so I had to concoct some story that somebody had pushed me.

Sylva Sheffield

A Coke Boiler

I started at West Leigh School in 1931 in Miss Gould's class. The boys' part of the school was to the west, the girls' in the middle and the infants' in the east. Our classroom had a coke boiler and the good children were allowed to sit near the heat. After one term, all the children living south of Western Road were moved to North Street School and some of us were quite upset about it – we had to go to a mixed school.

At North Street I remember Miss Cobley who played the piano; she taught there for a lifetime and knew everybody.

It cost four guineas a term to go to Westcliff High School before the war, but in March 1937 I was lucky enough to pass the scholarship exam.

There were several schools in Leigh that no longer exist. For example, Highfield College on the corner of Burnham Road, a boys-only boarding school with a red and black uniform. Beverley College, also a boys' school, was in Burnham Road. Tower House on the corner of Salisbury Road closed shortly after the war. When it became a children's home, I used to eat my lunch under their kitchen window and the girls who worked there would give me cocoa.

Donald Fraser

Miss Vessey's nursery school at 25 Dawlish Drive, mid-1930s. John Tyler (front) remembers, 'Miss Vessey told my mother: "I don't know what to do about John – he doesn't want to play, he wants to learn".' (John Tyler)

John Tyler in his new Caedmon House,
Pall Mall, uniform, photographed by his front
door in Madeira Avenue, *c.* 1936. (John Tyler)

I Am, I Can, I Ought, I Will

I liked my school days at North Street School, where the motto was, 'I am, I can, I ought, I will'
and the colours were blue and yellow. For Empire Day, we'd make bonnets out of crépe paper
and dance round the May Pole while a girl played the violin.

At other times, anyone who played the piano was allowed to play a march while we
marched into the hall for assembly and prayers. I played 'The Soldiers' March'.

When I was there we were mixed until you were ten, then there were three boys' classes and
three girls' classes, which were kept separate with a railing in between the playgrounds.

In the snow we made slides in the playground – it was like glass but no one broke a leg! In
the summer the boys worked on the school allotments.

Miss Lawley was my last teacher: a very good teacher. All the teachers were 'Miss';
if anyone married they had to leave. We were certainly taught the three 'R's very well and
now, at ninety-one, I challenge anyone to a game of Scrabble or Bridge!

Before I left school I took evening classes to learn shorthand, typing and bookkeeping
because I wanted to work in an office. However, when I left, aged fourteen, my mother
advised me to get a local job so I could go home for dinner, rather than go up to London.
Well, you listened to your mother in those days.

Ruby Frost

Where Do I Live?

Pat Bailey in North Street School uniform, 1950. (Pat Bailey *née* Humphress)

Starting school in the late '30s was not a happy day. We had recently moved to Oakleigh Park Drive and, as we set off for school, some workmen came to remove the 'For Sale' sign. I cried all the morning, not because I didn't want to be at school but because I didn't know how to find out where I lived. Of course, Mum came to collect me, so it was all right. When we got home, we put the white card with a large blue 'W' printed on it in the window, so the Wall's Ice Cream man would stop. He cycled round the streets on a tricycle with a big box of ice cream in front, looking for the cards and ringing his bell.

After that, I was happy at school – a small private girls' school, Queenswood, on the London Road (now a wine bar). Our uniform was brown, yellow and green, yellow blazer with a green 'Q' embroidered on the pocket and a matching beret. Extra activities were plenty – our own Brownie pack, tennis with half-size rackets for the smaller ones, elocution lessons, etc. For gymnastics, we marched in a crocodile about half a mile along the London Road to the Arlington Hall at Chalkwell. Playtime games were seasonal, with tops, hopscotch, marbles and hoops. Deportment was important: after morning prayers, we lined up to march back to our classrooms to music, with our books on our heads. If one was dropped, the unlucky child had to start all over again.

Doris Williams

Intense Prayers

My journey to West Leigh School was down Bailey Road, along Eaton Road to the house with the rabbits and chickens, and then along a little alley that brought us out at St Margaret's Church. Then we'd go up to the London Road and along to West Leigh, which I thought was a very good school.

Mr Gibbs was the headmaster. He stood on a box for assembly every morning and would get very intense during prayers and very red-faced; he had brushed-back hair and the bit at the front would shake – but he was a jolly good headmaster. You stood to attention when he came in.

At lunchtimes, my grandad, who lived in Manchester Drive, would collect us and we'd walk home for lunch – a proper hot cooked dinner – then we'd walk back to school again.

Ellen King

Madeira Cake

In the '30s, Eastwood School was just a single building with a porch opening into the one big schoolroom, with a corridor behind it. From the corridor you could get to the room for coats and the headmaster's house. I was once sent with a message for the headmaster, Mr Gascoigne, and I timidly tapped on the door. Eventually, I went back and said there was no answer. The teacher came storming through and banged on the door and it opened immediately.

The toilets were in a separate block with no roof, quite a way from the school, just inside the railings. The road itself was much narrower then. When I was a pupil there, one of the gypsy girls fell on the school step, broke her wrist and immediately ran home. Within minutes gypsies started arriving at the school and surrounded it, and the teacher locked the front door. Then all the mothers began arriving to collect their children at the end of the day. When there were more mothers than gypsies, the teacher opened the doors and we all went home.

Miss Picken was the infants' teacher – we called them 'the babies'. There was also Miss Morton. The rule was that if you were married, you could not be a teacher, but they made an exception if you were a First World War widow.

At break time, the teacher would put a kettle on the big black stove, which was all we had to heat the room, to make a cup of tea. She would sit on a tall chair by the stove eating a large slab of Madeira cake. On rainy days when we had to stay indoors, we children would sit and watch the cake get eaten and drool.

Tom Mayhew

Late Every Day

One of the best things about Chalkwell School in the '30s was Miss Oliver – everyone loved Miss Oliver. The headmaster was Mr Curtis; he really liked me – he was always giving me the cane.

My brother was born on Empire Day: 24 May 1933, and everyone took little Union Jacks to school that day. I came home and told my mum that everyone was celebrating my brother's birthday.

In '38 I went up to senior school – Fairfax. I walked along the brook to get there and was late almost every day – attendance: good; punctuality: poor.

Early in the war they had these things called group schools, where a teacher came round and you had a couple of hours' tuition in people's front rooms. Miss Oliver always came to my mum while I went to one down the end of Surrey Avenue.

Eastwood School Christmas party, 1933. (Tom Mayhew)

Children photographed behind Eastwood School, 1936/37. (Derek Barber)

Then in late '39/early 1940, they took Fairfax School over as an emergency hospital and shunted us and all the teachers back to Chalkwell – I don't know how they fitted us all in! The last day I went there was 31 May 1940 and we were evacuated on Sunday 2 June.

Denis Kirby

Flooded Stairs

I began my schooling at Chalkwell Infants School in 1945, soon after we'd moved to Kent Avenue. Boys and girls were kept separate: boys upstairs, girls downstairs. There were two playgrounds out the back, east for juniors and west for infants, plus a grassed area, which now has buildings on, and the toilets were out there too. I walked to school every day, then home for lunch and ran back again in the afternoon.

I once arrived back at school after lunch and found a tap was dripping into the long trough basin that went along the back of the upstairs cloakroom. I went to turn it off, but the tap came off in my hand – the boys had obviously been messing about with it. Water gushed out: all across the cloakroom and down the stairs! Halfway down the stairs was the headmistress's office, and she wasn't best pleased to have water pouring into her room!

Mike Grimwade

Chalkwell Hall, 1920s

I started at Chalkwell Infants School in September 1920 when the headmistress was Miss Mann. At first we threaded beads and had cardboard shapes to colour. Then we learnt to write letters. Numbers, adding and subtraction were learnt with the help of a counting frame.

On Empire Day, 24 May (Queen Victoria's birthday), we had a school tableau and a march past to salute the flag, followed by a service in the playground. In the afternoon, sports were held at the Jones sports ground. R. A. Jones, a school governor, came to the school from time to time with bags of sweets, which he distributed to each class and which were much appreciated.

One winter morning when I was still in the infants' school, we had had a very heavy fall of snow overnight, but I insisted on going to school, trudging along the middle of the London Road, no traffic about at all, and arrived only to find I was the only one of my class and was promptly sent home.

There were no school dinners; we all went home for a hot lunch and I walked both ways to Lord Roberts Avenue and was given 1*d* for sweets on the way back to school. A penny would buy an ice-cream cornet or four sugar sticks, several aniseed balls, or two sherbet dabs or gobstoppers.

We sat in desks for two, set in blocks of five or six rows on wooden steps running the length of the rooms, allowing everyone a clear view of the blackboard. Every morning we started with assembly, including prayers and hymns. We had lessons in writing, grammar, spelling, dictation, composition, reading, poetry, arithmetic, history, geography, drawing and painting, nature study, scripture, needlework and handicraft, and games. We had drill once a week, sometimes outside in the playground, and also played netball.

We wrote in jotters and best books. We enjoyed needlework and made samplers, dresses and nightdresses. In the playground (boys and girls separated by a yellow brick wall) we played hopscotch, skipping and exchanged cigarette cards. The boys played conkers and marbles and tops. We used beanbags for games and also played rounders.

Each term we had a visit by the school nurse, who examined our hair. We also had a visit from the dentist. I wore black woollen stockings in the winter and a navy gymslip with a white blouse and a blazer in the summer, but not all children wore uniform.

Most of us went on to other schools at eleven, but those that did not left school at fourteen.

Vivienne Barker

Classes Small; Teaching Excellent

I started at Tower House School in 1931. Winter uniform for the girls consisted of a navy blue serge dress with shantung collar and cuffs and a red satin bow at the neck. The summer dresses were also made of shantung, which we wore with red blazers and panama hats.

The building had been purchased by Mr Thatcher, former headmaster at Leigh's National Schools and later North Street School. His daughters started Tower House School: Miss Thatcher and Mrs Cowan – both Froebel trained. In the middle '20s, a single block was purpose-built for the school with a second storey added later. The grounds were extensive and there was a tennis court on the ground where two bungalows and Wirral Court now stand in Salisbury Road.

Tower House dance class, 1933. Shirley Rowe says, 'Mr Daniels, who lived on the corner of Burnham Road, would come in his charabanc and take us to dancing classes at Arlington Rooms.' (Shirley Rowe *née* Clark)

Advertisement for Tower House School, 1937.

The classes were small and the teaching excellent – geared to the individual needs of each child. We worked hard in the mornings at arithmetic, English and spelling, and in the afternoons we had activities including needlework, Greek dancing and plays. While we did our needlework, stories and poems were read to us. The music teacher was Miss Harding, who led the excellent choir and percussion band.

The school won many awards and cups at both the Leigh and Southend musical festival, for singing, percussion band and verse speaking. There were a few boarders but most were day pupils.

At the outbreak of war Miss Thatcher evacuated the school to Malvern, and it never reopened in Leigh after the war.

Jean Hamilton

Lessons – loved and hated

I had little trouble with reading and writing at school, but with arithmetic it was a completely different story. I couldn't care less how long it took to fill a bath with water at a certain rate of taps running, or how much time it took a train travelling at x miles an hour to reach its destination, with stops of five minutes at so many stations.

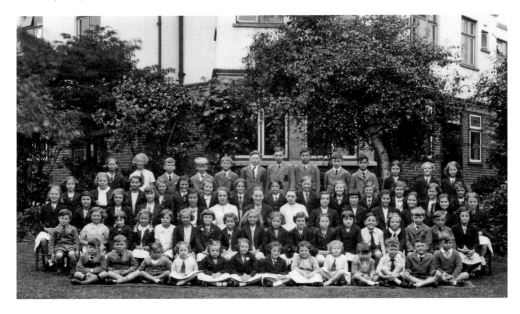

Tower House School which, as you can see, later accepted boys. (Ian Hawks)

Neither was I good at needlework. I was always the last to finish and then my garment was held up to the class to show them the wrong way of doing it. We made aprons, cushion covers, knickers (the old-fashioned bloomer type) and blouses. All these had to be cut out from our own patterns made up on graph paper. We even knitted dishcloths!

We often went for Nature Study walks and once were asked to collect as many varieties of berry as we could find and pin them on a big card. There would be a prize. The top end of Canvey Road was edged with bushes and so I found them a great source of berries of all sorts, which I thought would give me a good chance of winning. Alas, they were all disqualified as being of the ornamental and not wild variety.

One teacher, Miss Bradbury, was constantly looking out of the window at the Boys' Department in the hopes of seeing Mr Crowte, the love of her life, whom she eventually married.

Empire Day in May was always a wonderful morning of events in the playground in the '20s and '30s. We would all wear costumes of the country we were representing – the boys loved to black-up as Zulus – and sang all the national songs.

Other important events, such as the signing of the Armistice after the First World War, were remembered each November by two minutes' silence and we would write it in our exercise books, 'Today is Remembrance Day'. The teachers used to say, 'Thank goodness none of you children were in the war.' Little did they know what was coming!

Another event was the Silver Jubilee of George V and Queen Mary. We were each given a silver-plated tin of lovely chocolate, with the portraits of the King and Queen on the lid. For the Coronation of George VI in 1937, we had a book called *George VI, King and Emperor*.

I was seldom out of trouble at school for talking too much, and I watched horrified when one of our teachers, ginger-haired Miss Barnard, rapped my friend Betty over the knuckles with a ruler, spelling out each letter of the word 'I-M-M-E-D-I-A-T-E-L-Y' with a rap for every one because Betty had got it wrong.

Phyllis Jackson

Avoiding the Boys

Empire Day celebrations are my most vivid memory of West Leigh School in the '30s when the children dressed in national costumes and paraded on the grass area outside the school. There was May Pole dancing and a choir. I remember worn wooden floors and lines of desks, the separate boys' and girls' entrances, and the domestic science building.

When I was seven, I came home from school the long way round to avoid two boys who teased me and threw my beret over the hedge into someone's garden. On the way, I met Phyl Plumb, who was also avoiding boys, and we are still friends today. All summer we spent as much time out of doors as we could, either on the beach or in Belfairs Woods.

Thelma Nicol

West Leigh Junior School, 1930s. Back row: Jean Restorick, Eileen Clark, Madeleine Methuen, Eileen Cruchlow. Middle row: Joan Bundock, Joan Attridge, Elvina Morley, Jean Taylor. Front row: Betty Knott, Elaine Thompson. (Phyllis Jackson *née* Plumb)

A Rod of Iron

In 1943 I joined St Michael's School in Hadleigh Road, run by the nuns of the Order of Saint Michael and All Angels, as a weekly boarder. At seven years old, I had never been away from home before.

The school had been closed at the beginning of the war but reopened as Britain's initial invasion fears subsided. There were only about ten boarders when I joined but numbers were growing and the school was short-staffed.

Mother Lucy, who insisted on being addressed as 'Mother Superior' at all times, was in charge and, although very elderly and partly disabled by a stroke, ruled with a rod of iron. The three other nuns looked huge and frightening in their black habits and, in contrast, Revd Mother was very tiny and wizened, but even more forbidding. They must have had a hard time trying to do everything from managing the coke-heating stoves to cooking for the boarders on wartime rations and teaching, with a few part-time secular staff to help out during the day.

The uniform was navy, with velour hats for winter and panamas for summer. The indoor winter dress was navy serge with red binding. It had long, itchy sleeves and a matching tie and special indoor shoes. The summer dress was cream Tussore silk, worn with a navy blazer. We also had little grey, cotton gloves with buttoned cuffs.

A dread of mine was being the one to turn out the light in the dormitory and trying to find the way back to bed in the dark; and it was VERY dark with the black-out in place. Often, some joker would put something nasty in the bed.

We took a top blanket from home to personalise our beds and when the air-raid siren went in the night we had to go down to the chapel, wrap ourselves in our blankets and try to sleep on the pews until the 'All Clear' sounded. In the morning we washed in cold water, standing at the communal washbasins.

Breakfast was bread dipped in reconstituted dried egg and fried (actually much nicer than it sounds). One morning it was my turn to help serve and I dropped a slice off the plate I was carrying. The nun on duty told me to pick it up and have that one myself: food must not be wasted when there was a war on! I put the dropped slice in my place, only to be told by the other member of staff that it was very bad manners to serve myself first. So someone else got the dropped slice after all!

The number of pupils at the school was growing rapidly and the nuns found it quite hard to maintain discipline, and we boarders were not well cared for. There seemed to be little after-lesson supervision in the evenings and a lot of the girls were unkempt and dirty. I remember being severely reprimanded for having head lice, which seemed most unfair as I had caught them from someone at the school.

I was unhappy as a boarder. I went home at weekends and, in the end, I believe I cried so much each Sunday evening at the prospect of returning to school that I was allowed to leave.

Christine Selby

Wartime Education

At North Street School I remember Miss Callaway, Miss Cobley, Mr Harvey and Mr Morris the headmaster. I had not been there long when war was declared and they built air-raid shelters on the east side of the playgrounds but if the sirens went before school we didn't have to go in until the 'All Clear' sounded, so we used to pray in the morning that the sirens would sound so we could stay at home.

For a short while there was no formal schooling for us in Leigh and we were taught in people's houses, but we were back at North Street by 1942.

I started at Westcliff High School in 1945, taking the No. 21 bus from Rectory Grove to Middlesex Avenue; that's where we cribbed all our homework: on the bus on the way to school.

You had to play rugby for the first two years, then you could opt to do cross-country running instead. We ran across the A127, up a little path to Eastwood Church, left to Snakes Lane, then all the way back to Kent Elms Corner, across the 127 again to arrive at Elmsleigh Drive; then along what is now Blenheim Chase, which was just a field with a path; no houses there at all then.

David Flack

North Street sports team, 1952. Roger Rolph is at the back, fourth from left. (Roger Rolph)

Fairways Junior School, *c.* 1956. (Derek and Shirley Rowe)

A Shaky Start

I was desperate to start school. My fifth birthday was on a Thursday and my mother took me along to West Leigh. When we arrived, Mrs Rowden, the Head of the Infants, told my mother to take me home and bring me back on the Monday. I was bitterly disappointed but, now that I had seen what school was like, I wasn't very keen to go back on the Monday!

In the '50s, the youngest infants were taught in two temporary classrooms, known as the 'huts'. Each one was heated by a large boiler with a chimney going out of the roof. There was a railing separating the boiler from the desks and in wet weather all our coats, scarves and gloves would be draped over the railings to dry. The toilets were in the playground (you were only allowed to use them at playtime) and often froze in the winter. The caretaker, Mr Munt, usually managed to unblock them, but on at least one occasion we couldn't use them at all and had to queue up to use the staff toilets.

Dorothy Lewis

Berets at Belfairs

What I most remember about North Street School is my mum and aunt buying cakes at the Homemade Bakery in The Broadway and posting them through the school railings to us at break time. There were hot-water pipes in the classrooms and the teachers insisted on putting

Boys at Belfairs School, soon after it opened, *c.* 1955. (Roger Rolph)

our milk on the pipes to warm it – it was horrible! Mr King was the headmaster, and one of my teachers always had her hair up in a bun, held in with loads of clips.

By the time I went up to Belfairs, we were living at Kent Elms, from where I had to catch the school bus, which dropped us at the top of Hadleigh Road. My teachers always seemed to be calling out to me, 'Are you paying attention?' I hated wearing the horrible berets, which we whipped off as soon as we got outside school, although you'd get in trouble if a teacher caught you without it.

Pat Bailey

Games in the 1950s

At West Leigh, skipping was very popular, either individually or with a long rope and several girls (always girls) jumping simultaneously. However, jacks and fivestones were also very popular summer-term pursuits. Hula hoops were the fad of the day in about 1957, and came in different sizes.

The boys used to throw cigarette cards against the fourth-year wall. Marbles were a classic and much less dangerous than a game like leapfrog, when a line of backs was produced by each boy bending forward and holding the sides of the one in front. Then the boys would run and land as far ahead as possible on the backs.

But the real treat was when Mr Parslow allowed all-comers to play a bat and ball game in the lunchtimes, on sunny days. There was a square target that, if you missed hitting the ball, he almost always hit and that meant that you were out. I believe that we scored runs, straight between two stands.

On a snowy morning, my brother and sister and I used to head for school at 7.30 a.m. to be the first to run around the virgin snow. Only the caretaker would be there, stoking the boilers for the heating. If the snow fell at the weekend, we would head to the cliffs with our homemade sledges and spend hours trudging up the slope – only to go straight down again and land in a heap. There always seemed to be snow in winter and sun in summer.

I remember the freezing-cold loos in the middle of the school playground that were substituted by earth buckets in the deep frosts! Not very inspiring!

Averil Eve

Dropped My Cards

I remember myself as a lot of a nerd at Blenheim back in the '50s. I was the one who dropped his cards on the tram on the day we went to the school to take tests, was in the orchestra, read a reading at Christmas once, did a French recitation at a speech night, and ran cross-country because rugby was a bit rough and not because I wanted to smoke a few fags on the way round.

David Little

Catching Lizards

I enjoyed Eastwood School in the '50s. It was a mixed school but we had separate playgrounds: girls in the north-west corner and boys in the south-east corner. There was a canteen for school dinners in front but behind the school was all rough fields. We were allowed up there in the lunchtime and we went catching lizards – much to the girls' disgust!

In my latter years, some pupils were encouraged to have one of the allotments in our school grounds, but I was in the 'A' form and it was frowned on that I wanted to do gardening. I was in the cricket team, the football team and the basketball team. We trained in the gym together with the girls' netball team. Half the basketball team were dating girls in the netball team, with similar relationships going on between the gym masters and mistresses. Opposite the school were fields with footpaths where we did our cross-country running.

Mike Grimwade

Blenheim School, 1950s

I was at Blenheim School between 1952 and 54 and again from 1956–58, and remember the classrooms as very light and airy rooms. My teacher was Mr Potter and he was the nicest teacher you could ever wish for. We learnt the recorder and there was a school choir, and classical music was played in assembly. The school uniform was grey and red.

Heather Curry

Mr Weedon's class, Blenheim, 1959. Back row: Graham Knight, Donald Panrucker, Steven Parker, Tony Miller, Patrick ?, Graham Noakes, Paul Staines, Stephen Rapley. Second row: Keith Payne, ?, Lindsey Spooner, Janet King, Margaret Ross, Wendy Garrett, ?, Brian Faulkner, Keith Roberts. Third row: John Yeomans, Peter Scott, Stephen Perry, Michael Howard, Gary Cumberland, Derek Langley, Steven Bowman, David (John?) Burton, Richard Gray, Roger Gardner, John Chapman. Front row: Eileen Munro, ?, Janet Mansfield, Linda Payne, ?, ?, ?, Sally Mayall, Gillian Garrett, Lynn Gillett. (Warwick Conway)

Blenheim Junior School country dancing team, which took second place at Leigh Music Festival in 1961/62. (Warwick Conway)

Class 2, West Leigh Junior School, 1958. Back row: Janet Morris, Jane Evans, Barbara Lennard, Marilyn Fincher, Susan Anderson, Glenys Walker, Andrew Ditton, Clive Stone, Clifford Seagrave, Jonathan Higgins, John Gorrod, Geoffrey Hart, Pauline Elvin, Richard Neville, Alan Morris, Susan Bradford, Averil Evans. Chair row: Penny Harrison, Martin Hunt, Dorothy Nightingale, Jackie Foreman, Toni Lupton, Vivien Lale, Christine Dawes, Glenys Sewell, Janet Carrot, Helen Pickford, Glesni Chesher. Front rows: Trevor Pitkin, David Rodliffe, Leslie Shires, Paul Sand, Martin Phypers, Ian Thornton, Robert Wolveridge, Richard Phypers, Jennifer Croft, Valerie Trow, Mary Townsend, Gillian Martin, Christine France, Roger Norris, Annette Lay, John Smith, Stephanie Allen, Simon Andrews, Barbara Mussell, Anthony Everitt, David Rawlings. (Dorothy Lewis)

School Dinners

Few children brought up in the 1950s have happy memories of school dinners. They tended to be quite stodgy and soggy. I was so put off some things at West Leigh that I have never eaten them since: tapioca (which we used to call frogspawn), semolina, and boiled ham with pease pudding. You weren't allowed to go out and play until you had finished every morsel on your plate as, I suppose, there was a horror of waste so soon after the war.

We also used to have compulsory school milk. It was a small bottle, equivalent to a third of a pint. They would be delivered to each classroom in a crate and there would be a milk monitor who would have a special gadget with which to punch holes for the straws. I hated the milk because it never seemed very cold. Once I went to have a tooth out at the dentist's but there was no suggestion that I would have the rest of the day off. Back to school I went. 'At least,' I thought, 'I will have missed the dreaded milk.' No such luck. The teacher had warmed it up for me on the radiator as she thought it would be soothing after the tooth extractions! I have never been able to drink milk on its own since.

Dorothy Lewis

Three

BEACH DAYS AND
OLD TOWN MEMORIES

Old Town Memories 1910-20s

The cobblestoned High Street would resound to the clatter of steel-studded leather sea boots of fishermen as they made ready to go out in the small hours. These were stirring times for me as a boy going out with Father. Heaving up anchor and steering a bawley under full sail was an exhilarating experience. I learned much seamanship and felt as proud as any admiral on the quarterdeck of his flagship.

Bell Wharf was a busy centre in those days. The river would be alive with Thames sailing barges unloading cargoes of various kinds.

A little farther along stood 'Lumpy Cotgrove's' shop, a meeting place for teetotallers who would sit at the tables consuming mineral waters at 1d or 1½d a bottle, swapping yarns and playing dominoes, while in the window there was a succulent display of sweets at 4oz for a penny.

Next door stood a row of cottages, then Tomlin's Wharf where two-masted schooners discharged coals. Next to the Smack stood Juniper's fish shop, which was over 400 years old and added its picturesque charm to the character of the High Street. Next was the blacksmith's, where the huge dray horses were shod. They pulled railway and coal wagons up the hill.

The space which is now the Peterboat car park contained a shop and a row of wooden cottages. The building opposite was formerly a boat-builder's premises. Some years before the war, a bawley built there became stuck across the High Street in the course of its short journey to the sea. It had its bow against the upper window of the shop and its stern wedged against the walls of its shed, and there it squatted on its bilge and refused to budge until much brickwork was removed to enable it to be slewed round. During this delay, the tide had receded so that the Mayor and his dignitaries, in full regalia, had to leave without having performed the launching ceremony. Eventually, like a stranded whale, the bawley was launched into its natural element.

Archie Kirby

Leigh High Street, looking west, 1950s. Junipers is on the left.

A Close Community

I was born in 1923 in a two-up, two-down house in Leigh High Street. It was a very close community but my dad was never accepted in the Old Town because he wasn't born there.

Our house was set back from the road, with only a tiny gap between us and the railway line behind. We had oil lamps when I was young, but later we had gas put in. We had a front garden, but we children used to play on the Strand Wharf where there were five houses: three wooden ones and then two brick ones, with the toilet on the end, shared by them all, apart from the very end house that had its own toilet. However, they were lovely houses inside: quite big.

The three wooden houses had a big step down to get into them, like several of the houses along Leigh Street, so were often flooded. The people didn't think anything of it; they were used to it, but I've seen furniture floating around ... allsorts.

We were lucky that our house was never flooded. We didn't have to share our toilet either, although it was outside. Mother hung our washing out to dry in the front garden but the people who didn't have yards had their washing drying on a spare piece of ground opposite the conduit house.

Just off the Strand was Alley Dock where Theobald's barges came up, bringing timber. Two cranes on the end of Strand Wharf lifted the timber onto long carts. There was also a tumbrel cart that took sand to the Leigh Building Supply on the London Road by Leighton Avenue. To pull the carts, three lovely big old cart horses were kept in the Alley Dock stables, and when the tide was in they'd take the horses down in the Strand. I've seen the poor horses coming down Leigh Park Drive in the ice, sliding on their back legs. Brush's barges came to Bell Wharf; it was

Leigh High Street, looking west, 1930s. Just past the tearooms on the right, you can see Renee Horner's mother's washing blowing on the line in their front garden. (www.FootstepsPhotos.co.uk)

always busy down there. My sisters and I used to love seeing them come in and unload. And that's how I met my husband, because he worked on the barges.

On bonfire night, everyone got rid of all their rubbish and piled it up on Strand Wharf. As high as a house, it was. It was a wonder the old wooden houses didn't get burnt down!

There were many shops along Leigh High Street in the 1920s: Mr Bray's ice-cream shop on the corner of the Strand, Tom Shaw's baker's, a shop where Mr Thompson sold ice cream and smoked sprats. Joe Juniper smoked his own fish, too, and we loved to go down there and see him smoking them. The beach café was our post office, run by Mrs Cobley. Next door to us was Mr Kirby, an oil-monger, selling tar and paraffin – I'll never forget that lovely smell. The other side of us was Parson's tearooms.

At the bottom of Church Hill there was a haberdashery shop, a fish shop and a man who made baskets. There was a newsagent's on the corner, then a little sweet shop, a grocer's and a tailor's. On Leigh Hill we had Cotgrove's the butcher's and a slaughterhouse next to that.

Back in the High Street, Mr Shakespeare, who lived on the site of the teashop garden opposite the Peterboat, made glass eyes. Just beyond Shakespeare's, Frank Parsons built bawleys. When they were ready, they rolled them down the High Street on boat masts, taking the one out from the back and putting it at the front, all the way along, and then launched them from Bell Wharf.

I had a friend who lived on one of the houseboats. There must have been 200 or so houseboats, stretching from the cockle sheds, along past Johnson & Jago, nearly as far as Hadleigh Castle. Some of them were beautifully kept. Nearby was Theobald's farm; he used to take his cows over the railway crossing, to the fields owned by the Salvation Army.

View from the Cliffs towards the Essex Yacht Club headquarters, The Carlotta, 1930s.

The Peculiar People had their first Leigh chapel in Castle Cottage on Church Hill. Then they moved up to the chapel in Station Road. That building originally belonged to the council; it was then taken over by the Salvation Army and the Peculiar People bought it off the Salvation Army. I was the first baby in there, in 1923. And I got married in there.

We loved living down in the Old Town. Everybody knew everybody, and you never had to lock your doors.

Renee Horner

Half-a-Crown Return

Before the war it was half-a-crown for a return ticket on the train from London to Southend, so the seafront was very busy, especially at the weekend.

I had a friend who lived in Cranfield Drive, so I used to come down to Leigh a lot in the 1930s. We'd put our swimming costumes on under our clothes and walk down to the seafront. Mr Gilson would take us out on his boat and we would go swimming from the boat.

Freda Plimmer

Happy Holidays, 1925-1933

Chalkwell beach, a sand and shingle foreshore of some 500 yards, was divided into four or five smaller beaches by wooden breakwaters, each with a stone or wooden ramp, providing access from the promenade.

Chuddah Osborne and friends at the cockle sheds, *c.* 1930.

On the beaches at the eastern end, the Corporation would erect a row of tents. Beyond these stood a row of wooden bathing huts, old-fashioned even in those days, which the public could hire to change into their bathing suits. There was a small area of sand between the huts and the promenade, and here a minister from one of the local churches held a children's service every morning, with a portable altar and a little harmonium for the hymns. Children who attended regularly would be given a little medallion at the end of the week.

On the last of the public beaches, close to the breakwater separating them from the private Joscelyne's beach, was a large wooden hut, raised above the sand on piles, known as the minstrel's hut. On the landward side was a stage with a curtain that could be drawn back. Here, a small company of minstrels in brightly coloured clowns' costumes and with faces blackened with burnt cork gave morning and afternoon performances, singing, dancing, joking and performing sketches. At the end of the show, one of them would come round with a box into which you were expected to put a penny or two.

From each of the beaches, when the tide was in, a sailing boat used to take holiday-makers for half-hour trips. Just west of the Crowstone it was the *Peggy*, owned by Frank Bridge, a well-known figure in his dark brown jersey and thigh boots. He and his young crewman would arrive as soon as there was enough water for it to reach the bottom of the beach. Off went Frank along the shore. 'Come for a trip out!' he shouted. 'Sixpence each, half-price for children. Do you the world of good today. Half an hour, right out in the German ocean.'

Throughout the summer holiday, against the sea wall each morning, a newsvendor set up a pitch from which he sold papers, children's comics and a few beach toys. With every purchase you were given a numbered ticket and at the end of the afternoon there would be a draw for prizes, which usually consisted of nice but out-of-date children's annuals.

Thus would our holidays pass very pleasantly, my brother and I playing on the beach building sandcastles, sailing model boats, paddling, bathing or catching crabs while our parents sat soaking up the sun in their deckchairs and watching the constantly changing seascape unfold before them. On a rising tide the Leigh bawleys returned from their fishing grounds, some under engine, some still under sail, their nets hanging from the rigging to dry. Sometimes they anchored half-a-mile off shore, waiting for sufficient depth for them to reach their moorings in the creek at Old Leigh.

When we grew tired of beach, we could always watch the bowls matches on the greens behind the promenade or stand on Chalkwell footbridge until the next train came along. The terrifying chuffing noise, rapidly increasing as it approached, and the vast quantity of hot, sulphurous smoke thrown up to envelop us as the engine passed only inches beneath our feet, were not for the faint-hearted, and many lost their nerve and ran away. As one stood on Chalkwell bridge looking landwards (there was no station there at the time), the tall houses along Grand Parade stood out prominently and behind them the roads were all built on but, to the right, Chalkwell Hall estate had not yet been developed and was mainly open fields.

Geoffrey Brown

Thin Legs Waving

We had a beach hut at Chalkwell before the war where we spent a lot of time with Auntie May and Uncle Morris who would take us out on the water, with a little dog, Judy, sitting on the top of the boat.

Dad would come along at lunchtime for a swim and one of Mum's huge Cornish pasties. He'd stroll down to the water's edge with a cigarette in his mouth then, all of a sudden, he'd dive in and swim underwater all the way out to a raft; then he'd appear and pull himself up onto the raft and the next thing you knew, he'd be sitting there smoking his cigarette. He could also stand on his hands in the water; he was as thin as a rake and you'd see two thin legs waving above the water. Mother would get all het up and say, 'I wish he wouldn't do that.'

Wendy Newby

Beach memories, 1930s

There were three or four sailing boats down at the beach. On the first beach was the *Coronation*, sailed by an old boy called Billa Osborne. My dad used to mate for him at weekends, so I could go out free when they took people out on trips.

There was the *Albatross* on the second beach, owned by a man with a Hitler moustache. Mr Bridge, who owned the Bridge's grocer's by the Smack after the war, had the *Peggy* on the third beach. Then, down by the Crowstone, was a boat with red sails called the *Faith*, owned by Fred Ayres who was the bloke in charge of the yard at Johnson & Jago.

Chalkwell beach, with the Grosvenor Tea Room behind it, 1920s. Many Leigh families enjoyed Chalkwell beach year after year.

You paid 2*d* for a deckchair to watch the show on Chalkwell beach, but we used to sit on the wall for free and watch it. They had blacked-up blokes during the day and white blokes in the evening. I used to think they were black men.

We called the bridge next to Chalkwell station 'the yellow bridge', as it was always done in a yellow-wash paint.

Denis Kirby

Beach Tents

A big part of my life was Chalkwell beach. We had a tent which had to be erected each visit, a tradition which started when my mother was a child before the war. This continued all through my childhood and beyond, with every weekend from April to October spent on the beach. The weather had to be pretty bad for us not to go at least once at the weekend. The six weeks of the summer holidays were certainly spent there.

Janice Matthews

Learning to Swim

There was a level crossing at the bottom of Billet Lane where a signalman had a little hut and you could cross the railway line. However, a favourite game for some youngsters was to stand on the metal bridge by the Bell Hotel and try to spit on the last carriage of the train going through.

Leigh beach at high tide.

We all learnt to swim in Leigh Creek – a friend's grandmother had a cottage in the Old Town where we'd change into our swimming costumes. We'd follow the tide out, swim across the creek and then walk out to the Ray and swim across that. We'd also swim from the Strand Wharf. If the tide was in, you could have a boat ride from Leigh beach – quite large boats they were, that took about twenty people in each.

David Flack

Lovely Blue Sea

Before the war, Leigh was a lovely place to live and I had a lot of friends. After lunch at home, I would wear my swimming costume to school in the afternoon under my clothes, then we would go straight down to the beach afterwards to the lovely blue sea. We always sat in one particular part by a big boat.

Every summer, my grandparents stayed with us for a month. Grandfather had white hair and a great white beard. He was very dour and never smiled but came with us when we went down to the beach for the day.

Dad would stay on the train if he knew we would be on the beach and would get off at Chalkwell and then come along and join us. Mother would have his swimming things and he would love to go for a swim. Then we'd buy the most wonderful fish and chips from the shop by the beach and eat them as we climbed up the hill on the way home. Usually we went up Billet Lane, which was very steep.

Kathleen Young

Leigh beach with the railway station, left, and Bell Hotel, right. John Tyler says, 'I enjoyed standing on the footbridge over the railway – we ended up with faces black from the soot but that was all part of it!'

The 'new' Leigh station, far right. Donald Fraser remembers, 'While they were building the new station in the early '30s, a light railway was put up on Belton Way for the workmen's trucks and children would go down to watch them.'

Fun on the Mud

The beach was my favourite place, especially when the tide was in as we enjoyed swimming. When it was right out we could walk out to it. The first part was deep mud which was hard going, but when we got to the 'creek', which would be low at low tide, we came onto firm mud and it was easy walking. Then it was great fun, especially if there were others there and we had games. We had to watch out as the creek filled up behind us and we could have been cut off.

Wherever we were, we always had our picnic and a bottle of drink. Sometimes we were lucky and would see a 'Stop me and buy one' tricycle selling ice creams and frozen fruit sticks in card wrappers. If we were luckier still and happened to have a penny with us, we would buy one of the latter: Walls or Eldorado, if my memory is correct.

Thelma Nicol

Ginger Beer and a Packet of Crisps

Coming up from the beach, we'd get off at the bus stop at the top of Grand Drive – Mum, Dad, Grandpa, Vera and me – and if we'd been very good, Vera and I were allowed a ginger beer and a packet of crisps at The Grand. We weren't allowed inside but had to sit in the porch where there was a table and a wicker chair. That was a real treat: ginger beer and Smith's crisps for 1*d* or 2*d*, with the salt in a little blue bag. It was a lovely place.

Before the war, I sometimes went with Mr Harvey and his two daughters and wife when they took their boat round past Margate to rake cockles. We left with the tide and came back

View south from Marine Gardens towards the houseboats, early 1930s. Denis Kirby remembers, 'Twice a day, they'd bring the cows across the railway from Belton Farm, to graze on Leigh Marshes'.

with the tide, so it was a full twelve hours out. You would see the boats come back all in a line, follow-my-leader down the creek, to the cockle sheds.

Cockles were tuppence a plate from the sheds at Old Leigh. Coming back from the cockle boat, I'd take home a whole muslin full, freshly cooked. My mother would put them in a nice glass bowl and we'd have a cockle tea.

Derek Rowe

My First Boat

We moved to Kent View Avenue in August 1934 when I was just fourteen. Three days later, I walked along the cinderpath, through Old Leigh, past the cockle sheds to the Dauntless Co. boat-building yard, went inside and enquired about the cost of having a boat built.

They told me an 8ft canoe with a double-ended paddle would be £3 7s 6d. It would be built of solid wood – plywood could not be used for building boats because, in those days, waterproof glue had not been invented and it would just de-laminate in water. It would have a cockpit with room for two, the side would be painted pale blue and the deck varnished, the flat bottom coated with a black bitumen paint and there would be floorboards to sit on. I made a quick mental appraisal of my resources and found I could just manage to scrape together enough money, so I grandly placed the order.

The proprietor became very affable, said I would be most welcome to come and watch it being built and asked what name I would like painted on the bow. I was flummoxed for a moment, then remembered our dear old dog, Peter; I would commemorate him and call my boat *Peter*. Construction took about ten days and I had to find an extra 3s for painting the name. Luckily, another Saturday's pocket money just covered the cost.

Leigh promenade, with deckchair man, ice-cream man and boat trips, 1950s.

I duly took possession of the canoe and paddled it along to Chalkwell beach. The boat was much admired and everyone had a turn at taking it out and paddling it round the Crowstone.

Geoffrey Brown

Cockle Boat Breakfast

My grandfather and my dad (Henry), his three brothers and three sisters were all born in the Old Town. Grandad had his own coal business down there at the end of the nineteenth century and Dad was in the merchant navy and on the old sailing ships. I was the fourth of six siblings.

There was a coalman's yard by the station where they sold coals to the cockle boats, for a fire on the boats to cook their breakfast and in the huts to boil the water for the steam to cook the cockles. There were two big sailing ships down on the front, one for the yacht club and one for the Scouts.

I used to go down Leigh to The Ship on a Sunday morning for a drink with my father and brother-in-laws, from when I was about fifteen. Billet Lane is quite a hill and at the bottom was a kissing gate and you had to walk across the rail to get to the Crooked Billet.

Harry Bayford

Cockle sheds, 1920s. Phyllis Jackson (*née* Plumb) remembers, 'The smell from the boiling cockles was ghastly and I always used to hold my nose and run by as quickly as possible... I would slide down the mounds of discarded shells at the back of the sheds and arrive home with torn and filthy pants'. (www.FootstepsPhotos.co.uk)

Landing the cockles, 1920s. Kathleen Young (*née* Kidd) says, 'I liked to watch the sailing barges at Bell Wharf at high tide; it was a very important trading area, but was never the same after the war.'

Customs Officer Cottages

When we were first married, soon after the war, we lived in a former customs officer cottage off Church Hill, backing onto the old school house. It was brick built with a kitchen, lounge and two bedrooms, and steps up to the front door, but was in dire need of repair.

There were seven cottages in the row. The Blakes lived in No. 7, the Osbornes No. 6, Kitty Blake No. 5, us, the Plummers No. 4, Clem Cotgrove No. 3, Iris Tate No. 2 and a man we only knew as 'Jack' in No. 1. However, they eventually knocked our cottages down and moved us all into council properties in Treecot Drive.

Mr Hart lived at the top of Church Hill and in the icy weather he would put salt down on it. However, one New Year's Eve, on our way home from a party, we slid all the way down the hill to our terrace. It was very dangerous. Another New Year we went to a party along Castle Terrace at the Osbornes', and what I thought was brown ale was actually barley wine. It was potent!

Our two boys spent all their time down on the beach and the whole family loved to swim in the sea. We'd come out of the pub and go straight in for a swim if the tide was up. Our local was the Ship, where Mr Learmouths was the landlord at the time.

At the end of New Road, where the road bridge is now, were four or five cottages known as Townfield Place, and there was a railway crossing at the bottom of Billet Lane where a railwayman sat in a box and told you when it was safe to cross. When the gates were closed at the level crossing at the east end of Old Leigh, you could cross by the footbridge opposite the end of The Bay (Bell Wharf).

Albert Plummer

Toot-Toot All the Way

I had an idyllic childhood in Leigh in the '20s and '30s, when so much was still unmadeup and traffic was light. One family with a stable at their house on the Marine Parade used to clip-clop about in a pony and trap with canary-yellow wheels. In the summer at St George's School, we'd have our lessons under an apple tree in the garden overlooking the sea. At 3.15 p.m. my mother would be outside with my brother and we would go for a picnic tea on the sands. To get to the beach, of course, we went along the cinderpath – not asphalted in those days but really made of cinders.

Ice-cream was brought to the beach by a man on a tricycle and delicious homemade custard ice cream was sold there by an old man who had a drum surrounded by ice and salt in a large tub.

There was a level crossing with gates and a footbridge by the Bell Hotel and another pedestrian crossing at the bottom of Billet Lane, with a stile, opposite the town gas works. There was a long wall onto New Road with a single door at the east end to the 'down' railway platform. One had to buy tickets from the office south of the line. One day in the early '30s, a boiler blew up while the steam engine was at the 'down' platform, killing one of the crew.

When newly married couples left on their honeymoon from Leigh station, their best man usually tipped the engine driver and he then toot-tooted all the way to the borough boundary! On Saturday afternoons, one could count the number of weddings that had taken place in Leigh.

A friend of mine, Kathy Ford, worked as my mother's home-help for thirty years from about 1925. Kathy's mother kept a café in the building now known as Juniper's, which sold cockles and winkles. One or two steps led down into the building, so it was regularly flooded. The

Train coming through Leigh, 1950s. Norman Crane remembers, 'When I started work in 1937 (at 25s a week, since I had matric) the quarterly fare to Fenchurch Street was £4 18s 9d. After the war, it went up to £5 6s 0d!' (Don Stoneman)

Looking east along Leigh High Street. Geoffrey Williams' mother's shop was here, opposite the Peterboat.

building itself had wide risers on the stairs and the newel post was a tree, still with its bark on, dating from the sixteenth century.

Norman Crane

Smugglers' Cottages

When I was given a month's leave from Egypt in 1944, I found that my mother had moved into a shop and flat opposite the Peterboat. She was friendly with Len Williams, the landlord, and I would serve in the bar when 'last orders' was called.

Mother's shop sold 'women's necessaries' and was a very interesting building. It had formerly been a series of cottages and still had four staircases, but just one outside lavatory, right by the railway line.

There was a line of cottages on what is now the Peterboat car park. You could go into the first one, go behind the fireplace, up a secret staircase and through to each of the six cottages, from the days when it was involved in smuggling. Much smuggling went on there. On that quay, there was a tunnel – they used to row the boats underneath and come up under one of the cottages.

Geoffrey Williams

A Better Boat

After a couple of seasons with a canoe, I began to hanker after getting a sail that would save me the effort of paddling, so I purchased a 10ft sailing flattie for £7.

I paid half-a-crown to rent a mooring at Chalkwell and nailed together two pieces of timber to form a cross, tied a short length of rusty chain to it and buried it 2ft deep at the appointed place. I needed a riding chain about 24ft long for the boat to swing on when the tide was high but this would cost a fortune which I did not have, so a rope would have to do. Down to the Old Town I went and into Mr Kirby's small chandlery, where I told him I wanted four fathoms of bass rope. He cut it off for me and put it on his scales. I was surprised to learn that rope was sold by weight. 'One and tenpence,' he pronounced. I tied it to my mooring root and fastened a metal can with a handle to the other end so it would float.

To get the boat from our front garden down to the beach, I mobilised all the children in Kent View Avenue – there were about eight of them ranging in age from seven to thirteen. I had made a trolley out of a short plank screwed to a roller skate and we managed to lift one end of the boat and push the trolley under it. Then it was all hands to steady it while we took it down the road to Chalkwell bridge, over the railway and onto the beach. It was a nice, calm day and the tide was high as I rewarded my crew by taking them in two groups out for a row. They all went home while I rowed to my mooring, picked up the can and made the rope fast to my belaying pins. I sat there proudly until the tide had fallen sufficiently for me to wade to shore.

When high tide was in the late afternoon, my mother would pack a picnic basket and with her, my brother and our big black retriever dog, Jock, on board, we would sail along the shore. Past Chalkwell station, the cinderpath, Bell Wharf and the cockle sheds we went and on, up Leigh Creek until we came to an old hulk, *Violet*, lying at a crazy angle in a mud berth on Leigh Marshes. As the tide came in, the water rose inside her as well as outside. Tying up alongside, we scrambled up the steeply sloping deck and sat in a row on the gunwale. Jock's paws slipped so we had to reach down and haul him up by his collar. There in the peace and quietness of the marshes we had our tea and sat awhile, before sailing back to Chalkwell.

Geoffrey Brown

A Cottage by the Chapel

Soon after the war, me and my husband moved into a cottage near the little chapel in New Road, Leigh. It was a lovely place with a view right over to Canvey Island and Kent. When I went to the Wednesday coffee mornings in the chapel schoolroom, our cat followed me; she sat in the corner of the room, watching me have my coffee. When I was ready to go home, we both walked out together.

The wild geese used to come in every autumn and stay opposite my house. They came pretty well on the exact same date every year – all the way from Russia to Leigh.

Billet Lane was a bit steep! Before they put the handrail up – ooh! But there was a time when I could run up and down it, although I know a man who fell down it once and broke his leg.

One day my husband said, 'I'll teach you to swim.' So we went down to the beach by the cockle sheds and got into the water. 'That's it,' said my husband, 'you're swimming!' and he let go of me. Down I went! If he hadn't said that I would have done it. Everyone else in our family could swim – even the dog! And I still can't swim.

I began work at the Smack Inn. I'd walk there to open up in the morning and say 'hello' to the railway keeper at the level crossing on the way. At night, I'd lock up and then walk home in the dark.

The Smack got a bit rough on a Friday night when the hooligans came down. If they started throwing anything we worried about the bottles getting broken, and a police wagon sometimes parked on the hill in case things got out of hand.

The police often came into the pub at closing time in the afternoon and had a chat with us, and sometimes they gave us a ride home – I don't know what the neighbours thought: us coming home in a police car!

When I was there, in the 1950s, the Smack had a fish tank on the veranda and rats everywhere. The Old Town was infested with rats. We had one particular barman who was afraid of them, and if he had to go down to the cellar he would take a little bell with him and ring it as he was going down, to frighten the rats away. When we closed up in the evening we could stand at the end of the bar and watch all the rats come up from the cellar.

Connie Satchwell

Tea Gardens

In the '50s, in the three cottages beside the foundry (now Lynn Tait's) lived Mrs Harrington, Cissy Ford, and then Jenny Wiffon in the end one. There was one toilet and one tap out in the yard shared between the three cottages.

The café on the corner of Strand Wharf sold whiteweed. A lot of boats used to collect the weed, then dye it. They sold a lot of it to America where they used to line their graves with it. Mrs Dolby, who ran the shop, lived in half of the Customs House with her husband, a station porter.

Where The Boatyard restaurant is now, was a thriving boatyard. They employed nine or ten people, which was a lot for the Old Town, and they had a shop where they sold tools, nails, hardware and beautiful sweaters – everything for fishermen.

The current ice-cream shop was a grocer's. They'd take your order on a Thursday and deliver it on Friday. Beside that was a café and then the car park, half of which was taken up by a huge corrugated-iron roof under which the fishermen spread out their nets to dry, or to mend them when it was raining. The owner spent more time in the pub than at work and his wife would regularly ring the Smack and ask, 'Is he drunk yet?' If the answer was 'Yes', she'd say, 'Right, put him in a taxi then.'

The tea gardens opposite the Peterboat was originally our private garden. In 1979 I applied for planning permission to use it to sell teas. Permission was granted just three days later, so I rushed out to buy some second-hand furniture and the business took off – whoosh! We'd sell ploughman's lunches, homemade pies, scones and jam and cream. I did that for five years before going back to teaching.

There was a big crane on Bell Wharf where large ships would come up to unload timber. The crane driver, Billy Reed, once let his son, Danny, unload a ship and he tipped the crane over. The timber lorries were the only big vehicles we had down here in the '50s.

Irene Reynolds

Above: Leigh–on–Sea Salvation Army band. John Tyler says, 'The band often played on top of the shelter on Leigh Cliffs on Sunday mornings, and it was very pleasant walking in the gardens and hearing them.' (John Tyler)

Left: Phyllis Maynard. fourteen, and Ruby Loveland, sixteen, at work in Johnson's toy shop on the corner of Elm Road and The Broadway, 1935. (Ruby Frost *née* Loveland)

Chapter Four

OUT AND ABOUT

The Leigh Landscape, 1920s

In the 1920s, the Marine Parade and gardens extended as far as Canvey Road. There was a bank at the top of the cliffs opposite Canvey Road that was positively infested with glow-worms – a wonderful sight! Beyond Canvey Road was an arable field stretching to the position of Thames Drive and then another reaching to where Tattersall Gardens is today. The land between Marine Parade and the London Road was in the process of being built up, while the area between Crescent Road and Tattersall Gardens was not built upon until the '30s.

There was no Belton Way, just elm-tree hedges dividing the cliffs into fields with cows in, and Belton Hills farmhouse. Western Road was not made up; in fact, a stream ran along it, flowing east to Pavilion Drive, where it joined the Prittle Brook.

Marine Parade was well-named because on Sundays people put on their best clothes and paraded along it; there was much more walking done in the 1920s and '30s. H. G. Wells lived on the Marine Parade with Anthony, his illegitimate son by Rebecca West.

Mop-haired Mr Daniels lived on the London Road on the corner of Burnham Road and had a charabanc with which he ran mystery tours out into the country. I can't remember the trips ever

Marine Gardens, 1937. The gardens were originally fenced in, with metal gates.

Belton Hills steps,
c. 1935.

going beyond the River Crouch and they always seemed to arrive for tea at Hullbridge – then a tiny riverside village. Later, Mr Daniels and his brother acquired two splendid motor-coaches which were regularly used by school cricket teams going to away-matches.

The Highlands estate was all orchards, with a wonderful pond down by the brook Some friends moved into their new house in Buxton Avenue in 1938 but the land near the Nature Sanctuary was not developed until after the war. Although the map of Leigh did not actually have 'Here be Dragons' inscribed on its borders, one's visits to friends' parties in Tennyson Close or Olive Avenue required the company of one's father after dark to the safety of Grange Road. This was particularly so on visits to a friend in Bellhouse Lane beyond the Woodcutters, which was really the equivalent of a journey to Outer Mongolia, although Outer Bohemia would perhaps be more appropriate since what is now Bohemia Chase was the site of a gypsy encampment.

There was a large pond by Belfairs Farmhouse, a clay path through the woods to Daws Heath and a lot of anthills in Belfairs Woods. My mother once sat on one and was bitten so badly that she had to be wheeled home in my brother's pushchair.

The woods seemed much larger then, with spinneys and trees encroaching onto what is now the Highlands estate. The scrubland there was great for camping and hiding and tree climbing activities – wonderful for small boys!

Norman Crane

Impressive Sandcastles

On Joscelyne's beach there was a concert party held on a platform built out over the mud. We used to throw mud at each other and cover ourselves completely because we thought it was good for us. When you walked out when the tide had gone out, there was an impressive display of sandcastles.

I remember the Leigh Pottery brickfield in the 1930s as just a bit of open ground as it was not being worked then. Then the Corona cinema opened about 1932. Dad's shop always

Highlands Boulevard, 1950s. Joy Perkins says, 'The apple trees down Highlands Boulevard show where an orchard used to be.'

advertised the programme, so I got free tickets for the Corona. It just had one floor that sloped down and you sometimes had difficulty seeing the screen through all the blue smoke from everyone's cigarettes. There was always a rush for the back seats. Before the war, admission was 9d or 1/3d.

Arthur Perkins

Try Our Hand at Bricklaying

During the 1920s, Hadleigh Road and Leigh Park Road were quite busy with horses and carts going up and down with loads from Bell Wharf in the Old Town; coming up the hill, they hitched two extra horses on the front to help get the load up the steep hill. The fields behind the Marine Parade were all rough, with no Belton Way or station. Along Marine Parade it was usual to see Laurie Street's grandfather in his pony and trap. The Marine Parade finished just the Leigh side of Canvey Road and the field below was full of toboggans in snowy weather.

Two school friends, Mary and Diana Rowe, lived at the top of Canvey Road, the first road to be built on the new estate. When we went to play with them, we had to go through a five-barred gate between Harley Street and Canvey Road, which had a 'Private' notice on it. Building was going on apace and we liked to watch the men pushing metal barrows on rails with the building materials, and try our hand at bricklaying when they went off for their tea.

Joy Perkins

Flat Sprats and a Runaway Donkey

Mother had a wooden mangle but she had to get rid of that when my brother, Bert, then about six years old, found the sprats outside the back door. He lined them up along the roller of the mangle and rolled them!

Belton Way, with the 'new' station in the background. Donald Fraser remembers, 'In the '30s, there were several thatched shelters but never any vandalism.'

Dad had a donkey, which lived in our garden shed. When Bert was about eight, he found the key to the shed and got the donkey out. I was only six and Bert pulled me up on the back of the donkey behind him and told me, 'Hold on tight because I don't want you to fall off.' Then he took the whip and away we went!

We went right down Leigham Court Drive to the London Road, then across into Cricketfield Grove, which was then an unmade road. The donkey was running and I was screaming my head off. Someone who lived in one of the little cottages just before Manchester Drive came out and stopped the donkey and took us back home. My brother got the biggest hiding of his life and never touched that key again. When we moved house, Dad got rid of the donkey and cart.

Wyn Johnson

A Hair-Raising Ride

I was always one for 'the great outdoors' and used to plague my mother constantly when spring came, to get out of my thick, black, woolly stockings and into the freedom of ankle socks, saying all my school friends were into theirs. My next fight with her was to discard my liberty bodice and combs, and get into short-sleeved frocks.

Once the long days arrived, I would be over the cricket field at every opportunity to play with my friends, not at cricket but down by the brook, floating twigs, climbing trees and sometimes venturing a bit further on to Belfairs golf course and the woods beyond. We wouldn't come home until it was almost dark.

London Road, looking west from its junction with Cricketfield Grove – the site of Wyn Johnson's ignominious ride on a runaway donkey, 1922.

I remember quite a hair-raising ride once, with three of us on a bicycle across Belfairs golf course. John was pedalling with Betty side-saddle across his crossbar; I was on the luggage carrier at the back, hanging on to the back of John's shirt. Luckily, no one fell off, but if they had, it would sure to have been me in the normal way of things. I was fairly accident-prone: I was usually the one to fall in the brook, with my friend Thelma vainly trying to dry my stocking by whacking it against a tree.

Another time, we truanted from Sunday school to the beach with our dolls' prams and I suggested balance-walking on the breakwaters, although it was wintertime. The breakwater was about three inches wide and when I saw the water on each side of me, I panicked and fell in. I waded ashore with my clothes soaked. Again, Thelma tried to dry me, this time with a doll's blanket, but all to no avail. My mother was furious when we got home, not only for skiving off Sunday school or even because I lied and said I tripped over a stone and had fallen in (how was I to know some of our neighbours had been walking on the promenade and had seen what happened?) but mostly because she thought I'd ruined my navy blue nap coat with seawater. Fortunately and miraculously, after dry cleaning no stain appeared and she calmed down.

Phyllis Jackson

Newts and Blackberries

North of Suffolk Avenue it was fields all the way down to the Arterial in the 1930s. We often played over there – and got chased off regularly. There were five ponds there where we liked to catch newts, much to my mum's disgust. The farmer of Brickhouse Farm built a fence around one, so we used to go over and sit on the fence. Other times, we'd walk along the footpath that took us through to Elmsleigh Drive, picking blackberries all the way.

From Eastwood Lane [Mountdale Gardens] was a footpath that went down by some blackberry bushes and a riding school on the left. Opposite was a little lane with an old weather-boarded cottage. You ended up in a sloping meadow where Hurst Way is now. There was a ditch with a plank across, where we used to go on our bikes.

The brook was a favourite playground of mine and I often went home with wet feet. Before they built Darlinghurst School in 1967/68, that site was just an empty field where we used to play. During the war they built a public air-raid shelter over there.

Denis Kirby

Lime Avenue Fields

Children used to play out in the streets before the war, with our hoops, tops, bats and balls, but we were well-behaved and didn't cause any trouble.

Before Belfairs School was built, that was a vast playing field. We'd turn down Lime Avenue on our bikes, through a bit of rough wasteland (now Fairview Gardens), bounce over a hump and into the field. As soon as homework was done, I was out there, cricket

Mountdale Gardens, looking north, 1950s.

stumps, bat, the lot. That was our main recreation field then; we called it 'the Lime Avenue fields' and we were always over there playing cricket in the summer, and local clubs had football matches over there.

Later, I was in a band with Reg Johnson, whose father owned the toy shop on the corner of Elm Road and we used to go and practise round his house. I had a drum kit; Jack Clark was on piano, Reg on xylophone and a girl on accordion. We used to play at St James' hall for dances.

Derek Rowe

Sports Fan

As children, we played cricket in the street outside our house in Leighville Grove, using a tennis ball and trees as stumps. There were three old ladies who would look out for the ball going in their front garden and, if it did, they'd rush out and get the ball before we could. Other times, we'd cycle over to Belfairs to the site where the anti-aircraft guns had been. We had a mini-race track there and would race each other on our bikes.

One of my friends had a football, so we often all went round his house. We'd take the football over to Lime Avenue, across a bit of unmade road and through some trees to a huge playing

Leigh Rangers FC 1950/51. David Flack, Brian Turnidge, Brian Cannon, Stan Pace, Mike Ayers, Brian Phillips, Bob Flack, Billy Turnidge, Les Meddle, Cliff Haylock, Norman Baker. (David Flack)

Leigh Town Football Club at Belfairs Park, 1 March 1952. Behind them is the east side of Eastwood Road – the houses on the west side were yet to be built. (David Flack)

field. There would be any number of teenagers over there playing football, and Leigh Town Football Club played there. You could walk right across the fields to Brush's brickfields on the far side.

Tony Meddle was in charge of Leigh Town Football Club and he encouraged us to start a youth team, so they had some youngsters coming through. We were Leigh Rangers and later Leigh Town Juniors. We had to take the bus when we played away, or Mr Bridge would take us in his lorry.

David Flack

'Look Out Behind You!'

I liked to go over to the fields beyond Leigh station, towards Hadleigh where there were lots of little ponds. We'd go down there with jam jars and nets to catch newts, tadpoles and slowworms. Sometimes I'd take some home to keep for a while, and I sometimes took a slowworm to school inside my blouse and bring it out in lesson time. I also did quite a bit of tree-climbing with my cousin David and the local boys. We'd make our own bows and arrows and fire them at each other – it was great fun!

We used to run down Church Hill to see how quick you could run down without falling over. Then we'd go and watch the cockle men bringing the catch ashore in baskets hanging from yokes, and bouncing up and down as they came down the planks. They tipped the cockles into a huge square bath of boiling water, then sieved them with a big sieve and threw the shells out of the window onto the big heap behind the shed – it didn't smell very nice in the summer!

Sometimes we'd walk along towards Chalkwell to go swimming, crabbing or fishing with a bit of string in the paddling pool. When a train came along, all the kids would race across the bridge to try to be standing in the middle when the train went underneath.

Mum and Dad sometimes took us to the Coliseum where we sat up in the gods, and we thought it was lovely. It seemed very big. The Corona didn't have an upstairs but I often went on a Saturday morning with my friends. We paid sixpence to watch cowboy films featuring Roy Rogers or the Lone Ranger and enjoyed ourselves shouting, 'Look out behind you!'

Pat Bailey

Sticklebacks and Mushrooms

We used to go to Belfairs Woods and attempt to build dams out of twigs and small logs but were never successful. At that time, wild flowers were thick under the trees and the banks of the brook covered in grass.

On Leigh Cliffs we'd build dens out of broken-off tree branches. The Evans and Hooper families were out at 5 a.m. daily in the autumn, collecting button mushrooms from under the bushes on the downs and large flat ones from Leigh Marshes. We sold them to Edgeley's greengrocer and it gave us a good source of pocket money. In late autumn, we collected chestnuts from around the Hadleigh Castle area. Otherwise, we would catch newts and sticklebacks from ponds by the railway. We'd release them in our garden and, luckily, a neighbour had quite a large pond with a bridge over the middle, where the crested newts could breed.

We bought cockles in cotton bags and took them home to eat with brown bread and pepper. A few times, we collected winkles from Two Tree Island as, in the '50s, it was wild and undeveloped. We were once caught there in an horrendous storm with lightning and thunder, and sheltered under our beach towels with our clothes clinging to us!

Our family went to Chalkwell beach under the station walls and liked to build a sand boat before the beach became too crowded. We used to walk out to the Ray, a deep channel about a mile off the beach, to swim or run about on the firm sandbank. Swimming across was thought to be quite a challenge and we had to make our way back to the beach as soon as the tide turned. One day, my neighbour just could not pluck up the courage to swim a shallow channel on the way back and I had to pull her across. I was treated like a hero when she told her mother how I rescued her!

Averil Eve

Cornfield Walk

The first Salvation Army citadel, at the junction of Elm Road and Station Road, was taken over by the Peculiar People as a chapel and is now used as a nursery. My family belonged to the Brethren Assembly in Elmsleigh Drive and I went to the Crusaders in Lord Roberts

The Crusaders went on a cycle ride every Wednesday in the school holidays. Here they are in 1964 waiting at the horse trough outside the Elms to go on a ride. From left to right: Malcolm Scott, Keith McCullough, David ?, Bernard Wiggins, Barry Cornell, Michael Graves, Peter Smith, Ron Curtis and Julian Reid. (John Tyler)

Avenue. Later, we went to West Leigh Baptist Church in the building that eventually became the hall.

The original Christ Church was in Victoria Road but, in 1909, they put it on wheels and moved it up to Pall Mall, where they'd bought a plot of land. That building subsequently became the church hall when a new church was built. That 'new' building was in turn pulled down in the 1960s after the present church was built on the car park.

Evensong was held at the Coliseum in Elm Road because the church was so packed out. They'd take the Coliseum for evening services as the minister was very popular and had successfully built up the church.

Until the 1940s, Blenheim Chase ended just east of the top of Elmsleigh Drive, then there was a lovely hedge with a gap to get through to the cornfields. Half of Leigh would walk through those cornfields on a Sunday. On the north side of Blenheim Chase, there was an alleyway off Elmsleigh Drive also leading to the cornfields. In the opposite direction there was rough scrubland right across to Danescroft Drive.

Westcliff High School cross-country course went down a footpath with big hedges either side of it (now Treecot Drive), past the riding stables, over a stile through the fields to Cockethurst Close (which was then the name of the lower half of Bridgewater Drive) to Kent Elms Corner. Then up Eastwood Road North to Elmsleigh Drive and then back along Blenheim Chase through the cornfields.

John Tyler

Above: Joseph Hills'
cockle shed. Harry
Bayford says, 'The cockle
man used to come round
with a basket of cockles
on his head and another
on his arm, every Sunday
evening.'

Right: Christ Church in
its new position in Pall
Mall, where it was erected
in 1909. (John Tyler)

The original Christ
Church on the corner
of Victoria Road
and Cliff Parade. The
noticeboard indicates
that the vicar was Revd
Forbes Smith and that
Sunday evening services
would be held in the
Coliseum. (Roger Rolph)

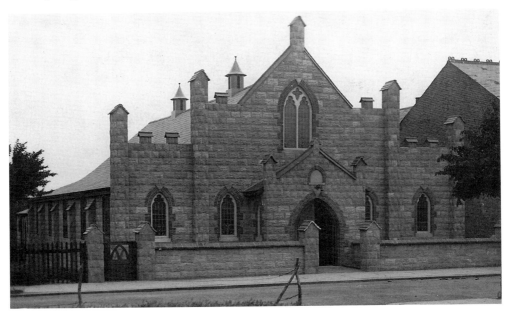

The new Christ Church building in Pall Mall, 1920s. This new building was substantially financed by Southend mayor S.F. Johnson. (John Tyler)

Town Landscape

My family moved to Burnham Road in 1928. At that time Marine Parade was made up as far as Thames Drive – the roads beyond that were built at the end of the 1930s. Belton Hills Farm was still operating – that didn't close until the electrification of the railway about 1963.

Beyond Walker Drive the roads were not made up, and neither were the Ewan Way and Buxton estate roads. Woodlands Park was not built until 1938. The Prittle Brook was open where it went under Highlands Boulevard. The boulevard itself stopped where the roundabout is now, with a footpath the only way to reach the London Road.

Every day, my father walked down Leigh Park Road and over the bridge, straight onto the platform of the old Leigh station. The railway goods yard was very busy in those days, and the tracks themselves ran all the way to the Gypsy Bridge, leaving only a tiny strip for the promenade. There was enough room for a complete train to stand there. There were several thatched huts with seating on the cliffs but, before the war, no vandalism.

Down in the Old Town, every space that is now occupied by boats and cars was a shop or a cottage. The cottages on Strand Wharf were knocked down in 1940. Later, building the 'road to the west' was the excuse for knocking other cottages down.

Donald Fraser

Kent Elms Corner

In the 1930s, the elm trees from which Kent Elms Corner takes its name were tall, stout trees growing just south of the Snakes Lane junction. They were taken down when the road was widened. We were frightened to go down Snakes Lane and would walk down the middle of the road with sticks at the ready in case we saw any snakes. Our shop was on the east side of Kent Elms. Opposite were clover fields, left fallow by the farmer for two or three years as they were to be sold for building land.

The A127 itself was a beautiful new concrete road with two cycle tracks to London, but the section running east from Kent Elms towards Southend was a more humble, two-lane road. There was an old Pest House, a former isolation hospital, on the south side of the A127 towards Southend: nothing more than an abandoned shack when I first knew it in the early '30s. Then someone bought it, did it up, and opened it as a café; we didn't like the idea of that. 'Fancy eating in the pest house!' we said.

Steam lorries with a coal fire and boiler and a funnel on the top would drive by, and we children would run after them shouting, 'Daft old lorries with your nose sticking out!'

Before Perry's was built, that field was a wonderful playground for us. A Goodman's horse-drawn furniture van had been abandoned there and we used to play on it a lot. There wasn't much traffic about, so it was quite safe all around there. However, a young friend of mine ran out and was killed by a city bus on the Rayleigh Road, which shocked us all. 'She was too good to live,' I overheard the adults say, so I decided that from then on I would be naughty.

Our Lady of Lourdes, Leigh Road. Phyllis Jackson was married at Our Lady of Lourdes on 22 September 1945, followed by a reception at Jeanne d'Arc Café on the London Road near Thames Drive.

Bridgewater Drive only went as far as the shops, then it petered out into pasture for sheep and cattle on the steepest section. There was a brook with a plank across for access, and Tibbenham's Dairies on the east side. Meanwhile, Cockethurst Avenue was built up from the A127. Eventually, the roads were continued through to join up and became Bridgewater Drive as we know it today.

Tom Mayhew

Treecot Farm

They started building Treecot Drive from the Bridgewater Drive end – the top end was still muddy fields when we moved in, no road there at all. At that time, the early '50s, the A127 was very little used: there was hardly anything on it.

Originally, there was a pond in the middle of this area and, after they'd built the houses, they had to pull three of them down because they'd been built on the pond. When we first moved in, you had to go up and get your own earth for the garden, which they'd left in a big heap at the top of the road.

Albert Plummer

St Edith's, Hillside Crescent. Poor families would come here for holidays in the '40s and '50s. Marian Cove became friendly with one of the nuns, Sister Josephine, and says, 'She was allowed to come into our house but was not allowed to have a tea or coffee.'

Belfairs bowling green, 1950s.

Muddy Fields and Bomb Sites

The site of Darlinghurst School was fields – very muddy fields. That was our play area around 5 November, when we put bangers in apples, bangers in potatoes, bangers in anything we could find!

Another great play area was the ruins and foundations of the houses on the corner of Manchester Drive and Pavilion Drive that were bomb-damaged in the war; we were always in there.

Brickhouse farmhouse, quite a nice building, stood on the site of the present fire station. We had great fun playing in its cornfields and I remember the harvest gathered in by horses and wagons. Behind the farm we liked to sneak into the barns, climb trees and jump onto the haystacks.

The huge fenced-in pond was superb for catching newts and salamanders in nets and jam jars. Another pond, further west, had the famous cross trees. You had to climb a tree on one side of the pond and get from that tree across to the other side of the pond on the other tree. It was known as 'the cross tree pond'.

In 1951 we all got bikes and we'd ride down to Leigh and along the sea wall or go down and swim out to the mud. As we got older, we'd go over to Cornish's brickfields behind the Bellhouse, where we were interested in seeing the little train working.

In the mid-'50s, they built a lovely outdoor swimming pool at Westcliff High School for Girls and, on warm summer nights, we boys would bunk over the fence and have a swim. If a police car came by, we'd just keep quiet until it moved on. It was a very nice facility.

Mike Grimwade

The Two Sheriffs of Leigh

We were living in Station Road, Leigh when my brother, Alan, and I found a 10*s* note one day, about 1950. We were aged about seven (me) and nine (Alan). We couldn't believe our luck and off we went to Leigh Broadway to spend it. The first thing we got was a sheriff's badge and a set of guns each – we were the two sheriffs of Leigh. The rest was spent on sweets and cakes. When our Dad found out he was not best pleased and told us to go straight back and get the money back, so we had to take back our lovely guns and sheriff badges. We couldn't get our money back on the cakes though – we'd eaten most of those. It was disappointing to lose all our spoils, but we'd had a great day out of it!

Terry Fane

Cinemas

During the first half of the week, there'd be one film on at the Coliseum, then it changed on the Wednesday. The queues would stretch both ways along Elm Road. It was the same at the Corona round the corner, so you could see four films a week, if you had the money. There was also the children's show on a Saturday morning at the Corona – cowboy films and *Flash Gordon*. The dearest price was 2*s* 3*d*, or, right down the front, 1*s* 9*d*.

David Flack

Corona Cinema

During the interval at the Corona, they used to come round with a spray, disinfecting the air. They had a container on their back, with a long arm, and would spray the air. I knew a man whose job it was. He once got in to trouble for doing it while the film was still on and made everyone sneeze – you were supposed to wait till the lights went up, then everyone could get their handkerchiefs out.

Harry Bayford

Corona Chums' Club

I went to the Corona on a Saturday morning for sixpence, as one of the Corona Chums' Club. The manager, Mr Craven, would come out with a mirror which he'd use to reflect a spotlight onto the audience. Whichever child he stopped on would win a prize. He also had pockets full of sweets to throw out into the crowd. We called the commissionaire 'Buttons' on account of his long buttoned coat; he would see us safely across the Leigh Road. I once came second in a competition at the Corona to have the most conkers.

Roger Rolph

Southend Carnival procession, just passing the Peter Varley Dance Studios on the corner of Broadway West and Elm Road, 1960s. (Reg Sims)

Southend Carnival passing Dean's electrical shop in Leigh Broadway, 1960s. Ruby Frost says, 'Before the war, Howard's Dairies' dance troop would dance all the way from Leigh to Southend in the carnival. We'd take chairs up to the top of Avenue Road to sit and watch them come by'. (Reg Sims)

Southend Carnival passing the end of Oakleigh Park Drive, 1960s. Wendy Newby remembers, 'We always walked up to the Leigh Road to watch the Southend Carnival. One year it poured with rain but the road was still packed with people'. (Reg Sims)

Coliseum Cinema

I went to the Coliseum cinema once to see a film about Douglas Bader, but my wife came over all peculiar when he lost his legs and we had to leave. I thought I would like to see the end, so I went back later in the week and bought a ticket for the circle. The whole place was empty, apart from one solitary person sitting at the front. I recognised him as Roy Reed, a wealthy member of my golf club. I went up and tapped him on the shoulder and said, 'You're sitting in my seat!' He was going to get up, until he saw who it was. So we enjoyed the film together and went and had a drink afterwards too.

The Empire, on the other hand, was a real flea pit. That's what we called it: 'the flea pit'.

Geoffrey Williams

Pittington House

Pittington House was a beautiful building; not too big – a lovely, typically English house overlooking Old Leigh. My sister would have liked to buy it when it stood empty in the 1950s and we often went over to look at it and imagine how it could be done up. But the council wouldn't let her have it; they pulled it down along with two rows of cottages and built horrible new flats on the site.

They were also going to pull down Theobald's Cottages in the High Street because they didn't have bathrooms or electricity, but I went round with a petition and stopped it. The council bought them for about £300 each and then sold them for £4,000.

Irene Reynolds

Smugglers' Haunt

Lapwater Hall was a huge empty house with a long corridor, with all the rooms opening off it. I loved to go there after school; my friends and I would go all over the house – not in the cellar though because that was full of water. There was a walk through the grounds that they told us the smugglers used on their way to Rochford, but I don't know how true that was. There were also rumours the house was haunted but we didn't care – but I wouldn't have gone in there by myself! In the end they stopped us going in because it was dangerous.

Joan Herbert

Lapwater Hall

In August 1946, my wife and I, on returning from war service, bought our first house: 9 Lapwater Close.

At the junction of Lapwater Close and London Road stood Lapwater Hall. It was already in a dilapidated state and I was told that it had been requisitioned and used by the army for some years but, by 1946, was empty. The army had not treated it well and no attempt was made to restore it. After a few years it was considered a danger, so it was pulled down.

The plot of ground became a wilderness and I wrote to the owner asking permission to create an allotment there for growing vegetables, to which he agreed. For about ten years, I cultivated a small part of it but it was an uphill task as the weeds spread into it from the surrounding land. We moved away in 1964 and shortly afterwards the site was redeveloped into a block of flats.

Geoffrey Brown

Waiting for Trams

In the 1930s, trams used to stop at the end of The Broadway and I used to wait to see them come off the rails, but of course they never did. When we walked up Lansdowne Avenue and Beach Avenue to the beach, I used to find a large pebble and kick it into the lines along Leigh Road and then wait for a tram to come along, to see what happened.

I loved going on the open-topped trams. Later trams had open bits at either end and a semi-circular seat where the stairs came up; I used to wait for ages for one of those to come along.

Denis Kirby

Stuck in the Lines

My grandmother took me right the way down to Thorpe Bay on the tram – lovely! It was a great treat to go for that ride but what I remember most about the trams is getting my bicycle wheel stuck in the lines while I was cycling to school – heck of a job to get out again!

Shirley Rowe

St Clement's Brownies pictured in the library gardens, mid-1950s. Brown Owl was Mrs Head and Tawny Owl was the eldest daughter of Father Head (no relation) who was then Rector of St Clement's. The two guides in the photo who helped run the pack were both called Barbara. (Janice Matthews *née* Barker)

Doing My Own Thing

When I was older, I loved to get on the open-topped trams because they allowed me to go off and do my own thing. It was 3d to get to Southend in the 1930s and it was wonderful sitting up the front on the wooden seats with their wooden backs. When the tram turned round, the back of the seat slid across, so you could face the other way. Then came closed-in trams and, after that, the trolley buses, which had to change the 'arm' over at Victoria Circus.

Ruby Frost

A Birthday Treat

My brother's birthday is in June and mine in July, and if one of us chose to take the paddle steamer to Margate for his birthday treat, the other would choose to catch the tram from Leigh. The tram went down Southchurch Boulevard and Thorpe Hall Avenue and then back to Leigh, and that was our treat. You could reach out from the top of the tram and touch the trees; all very exciting for a small boy.

John Tyler

Trolley Bus Sabotage

The trolley buses ran on a circular route from Victoria Circus along the London Road, then down Nelson Road, Fairfax Drive and back up Victoria Avenue. There was a turning point in Nelson Road, operated by a handle on a post, which switched the overhead lines and re-directed the buses down Silversea Drive. Most of the time they never used it, except when schoolboys pulled the handle down and sent the buses the wrong way. Then the driver had to get out his great big pole and move the lines back; it only delayed them a couple of minutes but it was a fairly regular occurrence!

Mike Grimwade

Trams and Trolley Buses

Trams were good old things but you had to be careful when you rode a bike by the tram tracks or your bike wheel would get into the groove and you'd come off. The trams started out by the gas works, came up by the Kursaal, along the main road and into Leigh where they turned round. They didn't actually turn round, they just changed ends: they just used to throw the back of the seat over to the other side, so they faced the opposite way.

Then they had the trolley buses, which used to run from Southend along Fairfax Drive. The trolley buses had rubber tyres, which was dangerous because you never heard them coming. The tram had iron wheels, so you could hear them.

Harry Bayford

A tram at the Leigh Church terminus. Joan Herbert says, 'It was a real treat to go on a tram, riding up on top – if it wasn't raining!' (www.FootstepsPhotos.co.uk)

Five

SHOPPING AND WORKING

A Toy Shop on the Corner

Before Broadway West was built in 1932, there was a large area of rough grassland there and I can remember a big tree trunk that we used to play around. When they built Broadway West and knocked down Dr Watson's house, he moved to a double-fronted house along The Broadway and opened a practice there.

I remember the iron pilings going in for Clement's Court; everyone was worried about it being built so near the cliffs.

I left school aged fourteen in 1933 and found a job at Johnson's toy shop on the Elm Road/Broadway corner. The shop had been opened by Mr Johnson and his son in the First World War and sold everything from toys to stationery, photographic equipment, leather goods and fireworks. There were four rooms upstairs – originally living accommodation – with one room used as a showroom for the fireworks, which had to be kept separate. Later, all upstairs rooms were used as stockrooms.

Most jobs paid 5s a week, but mine paid 7s 6d, so I was really pleased. I worked from 9 a.m. to 8 p.m. and from 9 a.m. to 9 p.m. on Saturdays, but I had every other Wednesday afternoon off. While I was there they brought in a new law that shops had to provide a seat for female assistants, which didn't go down very well with Mr Johnson.

Ruby Frost

Bobby on the Beat

In the '20s and '30s, Johnson's toy shop was on the corner of Elm Road. Mr Johnson was tall with glasses and always wore a black suit with a wing collar. You had to go upstairs to get fireworks.

Partridge's was the fish shop. Mr Brown, a huge but lovely man, owned the double-fronted radio shop near Woolworths.

Clarkes was on the corner of Leighville Grove and Rectory Grove, with tins of biscuits in front of the counter with glass lids that you lifted up, including one for broken biscuits. I once bought some toffee there, which was real tooth-pulling stuff.

Leigh Broadway looking west towards Alexandra Road, *c.* 1910. Pearl Plummer remembers, 'When George VI died, all the shops put a strip of black tape down the windows as a mark of respect.'

Dossett's came round with their van twice a day. One day, the man left the van doors open at the back and Betty, a young friend of mine, for some reason threw sand in, all over the cakes. Her mother had to buy all the cakes and Betty was made to eat one.

In Glendale Gardens was 'Diddums' the grocer's, Kirby's the laundry and Bridge's Dairy (Mr Bridge wore riding breeches and hard leather gaiters up to his knees). Harvey's fish shop was along there too and on the way home from Guides, along Pall Mall, I often called in for two penn'orth of chips.

There used to be a bobby walking round the streets in those days before the war. You'd always see him walking along The Broadway, every day – I can see him now!

Shirley Rowe

Wartime Shopping

Mother always went to the same shops, as they held the ration books for our family. We lived in Tankerville Drive and our first stop would be Mr Tibbles the fishmonger, whose name always amused me. Further along the London Road, Mum's worst fears were realised at Mr Beale's, the dentist, where she had to have an extraction one day and never went back again.

We would cross the road to our vet Mr Misselbrook, who cared for our cat when he got run over. Next door was Beaver's Stores, a general food shop where biscuits were displayed in glass-topped tins outside. We couldn't afford these and had to be content with the broken ones kept in the back of the shop and put into brown paper bags. I watched as the assistant cut out the relevant coupons for our weekly rations, and carefully weighed out very small quantities of margarine in greaseproof paper and a few ounces of sugar into a blue paper cone. I believe we were all allowed one egg each per week, which Mother supplemented with powdered egg to make cakes and puddings. Mr Rutter, the butcher, was visited next and he too took our coupons for the meagre ration of meat – usually cheap cuts which needed long slow cooking. I became very fond of tripe and onions, oxtail, stuffed hearts and all sorts of offal.

Another short walk would find us at Mr and Mrs Little's, the ironmongers, which we called The Oil Shop. Besides oil, they sold a variety of goods we would buy in places like B&Q today.

Vegetables would be on the list next but we were not able to carry potatoes at the same time as other heavy goods. Potatoes would be delivered by Mr Blanchard in his horse-drawn cart. He owned a smallholding in Eastwood and brought a selection of vegetables, flowers and sometimes fruit to the door. The milkman also delivered by horse and cart and Father always tried to beat our neighbours to collect the manure the horse left, for his allotment.

Annette Tidman

Leigh Broadway looking west from East Street, *c.* 1920. Wyn Johnson says, 'There two steps at the kerb in Leigh Broadway in the '20s, and my brother was told off for standing with one foot on the top and one on the bottom step'.

Dossett & Sons bakery, 88 The Broadway. After the war, there were two Dossett's in Leigh Broadway: one up by The Grand and one at the top of Elm Road. (Derek Barber)

Remembering the Brewers

My maternal great-grandparents, Edric Brewer and Annie Busby, were both born in Old Leigh where Edric's parents kept the butcher's shop and Annie's parents had the grocer's. When they married in 1884 they continued the grocery business, and in 1894 moved to the top of Leigh Hill opposite St Clement's Church which was, until quite recently, The Broadway wine stores.

In 1907, Brewer's grocer's shop and post office was built in Leigh Road and the family moved there. My grandmother married Edgar Rush and after the First World War he went to work at the shop too.

My mother married Reginald Barker at St Clement's Church and regularly arranged the flowers there until she found standing too difficult. For the last few years, they attended St James' Church in Elmsleigh Drive, which they lived next-door to. In fact, it was her grandfather, Edric Brewer, who gave the ground the church is built on and her aunt, Maud Brewer, donated the cross in memory of her parents.

Janice Matthews

Brewer's Stores on the corner of Leigh Hill and The Broadway, *c*. 1905. (Roger Rolph)

A Little, Round Chair

There were good shops in Leigh Road. Brewer's was a big family shop on the corner where we bought most of our groceries. They had two or three little round chairs with backs, so my mum could have a sit down. She would go up in the afternoon and Mr Brewer would serve her himself, and then she'd be in there for about half an hour, chatting. She chose the afternoon as the shop was quieter then. Mr Brewer's sister helped out in the shop and her husband drove the van for deliveries.

Marian Cove

Aniseed Balls and Barley Sugar Sticks

In 1932, my parents bought a tobacconist's at Kent Elms Corner between the Arterial and Snakes Lane, and named it 'Rendez Vous'. It sold tobacco and sweets but most of the income came from teas and cakes served to passers-by, who would sit at wicker chairs and tables out the front. Much of our custom came from passing cyclists who would buy ice cream, cakes, pop, ginger beer and chocolate bars.

Mum would listen to the weather report first thing in the morning and decide whether to order some ice for the zinc ice-cream maker. Two men would arrive on a horse and cart and unload huge blocks of ice in sacking with great big tongs. We'd hammer the ice to break it up, then pack it around the edge of the machine and pour cream and custard powder into a cylinder in the middle. It was really good ice cream! On a good day we could sell it all; if it rained we were stuck because you couldn't keep it.

The RendezVous café at Kent Elms Corner, east side of the Rayleigh Road, 1933. (Tom Mayhew)

I remember Fry's chocolate cream bars and Mars bars for tuppence; toffees, ten for a penny; sherbet dips, a ha'penny; gobstoppers, which changed colour as you sucked them; liquorice root, like chewing a piece of stick!; bonfire toffee, hard and brittle, and 'proper' toffee that had to be broken with a hammer. We also had acid drops, pear drops, aniseed balls, barley sugar sticks and dolly mixtures.

Dad had had great ideas for the place when we moved in, but by 1935 five more shops selling refreshments had opened nearby and we went out of business. Dad had to walk from Kent Elms Corner to the labour exchange in Southchurch Road, to collect his dole. He received 8s – and there were six in our family.

They built Perry's right up against our shop in 1935 and caused a damp problem in our wall. We moved away soon afterwards.

Tom Mayhew

A Dear Old Horse

When we lived in Theobalds Road after the war, the milkman would come by with his dear old horse, Nelly, and I would go out to talk to her while the milkman came in for a cup of tea with Mother.

We had bread and cakes from James' bakery, who delivered in a van. However, my friend and I used to cycle down to the Homemade Bakery in Broadway West on a Friday to buy custard tarts. They were the best custard tarts of anybody's and we'd sit in the library gardens to eat them.

Sylva Sheffield

James the baker with his van, near his shop on the corner of The Broadway and Alexandra Street, 1930s. Ray Warman remembers, 'James had another shop on the corner of Westminster Drive and had a van shaped like a loaf of bread.'

Twice Daily

Mr Potter, the milkman, came round twice a day pushing his hand trolley from Howard's Dairy. He was a lovely chap but seemed to me like a very old man; he was our milkman for years. The milk bottle tops were cardboard, and you had to press the middle of them to open them.

Dossett's the baker also came twice a day, as did Cotgrove the butcher, who had a horse and trap and an abattoir behind their shop in Glendale Gardens. Nearby was Harvey's, the coalman.

Coming down Marine Avenue and turning left into Glendale Gardens, the first shop was Harold White's barber's, where I had my first haircut – sixpence!

Next door was Bacon's newsagent's where we got our papers, sweets and fizzy drinks for a ha'penny, and Sergeant's grocer's/greengrocer's. Mr Sergeant always wore a brown coat and walked with his hands behind his back. There was an off-licence on the corner of Fairleigh Drive that supplied lemonade and ginger beer – you could get a quart of lovely ginger beer for thru'pence and a refund on the bottle when you returned it.

My mother walked up to The Broadway every day before the war with her basket on her arm. Early closing day was Wednesday but, otherwise, the shops stayed open until 9 p.m.

Derek Rowe

Leigh Broadway, looking east, 1930s. Phyllis Jackson says, 'I never liked being sent to the shops, especially if I had to ask for anything difficult, such as remembering "Evan Williams' Camomile shampoo" – a real mouthful! Mum wouldn't indulge me by writing it down.'

Thames Drive Parade

After the war there was a good selection of shops at the Thames Drive parade. Our grocer's was between Walker Drive and Sutherland Boulevard, and one of my jobs on a Friday night was to go with a basket and our ration books to queue up for our week's allowances.

Dossett's baker's was nearby and there was another baker further down who you could go and watch bake his own bread. Barclay's Bank was on the corner of Stirling Avenue, and Howard's Dairies was on the corner of Thames Drive.

Ellen King

Leigh Hill and New Road

When we moved to the High Street in the '50s, I could do all my shopping in the Old Town. On Leigh Hill we had a butcher, greengrocer, a cane shop where they made baskets (later taken over by Vic Ellis the artist) and a secondhand jewellery shop. Across from them, on the south side of the road, was a café, post office, dress shop, cobbler's, an off-licence and a junk shop. There was a bank in the building called Bank House and a café further up Leigh Hill.

There was always somebody staying at the Bell Hotel, although they weren't rushed off their feet. There were four cottages next to the Bell, where the car park is now. They were only tiny places, one up and one down, but I remember they all had lovely brass letterboxes, always beautifully polished.

Before Oscar's restaurant opened, that building used to make cotton dresses and aprons, displayed outside on racks.

Next to the Ship was another café, a barber's shop and a newsagent. The man that ran the newsagent's was blind and his wife lived in Bermuda. Further along New Road was another grocer's but New Road only went as far as the Methodist chapel. Past the chapel there was nothing: just a little lane going straight down to the station.

Where the flyover is now was a grassy area where someone sold afternoon teas from a little wooden hut, and two cottages west of the Billet. In one lived a man who used to walk down Southend High Street with sandwich-boards, telling people that 'Jesus Loves You'. In the other lived a lady who sold cockle teas in her front room. Those cottages were pulled down when the flyover went in.

Irene Reynolds

'Would You Like an Onion?'

The Leigh Co-op took up the whole block of the London Road east of Blenheim Crescent, but my mother preferred to shop in The Broadway. She always bought her greengrocery from Palmer's, nearly opposite Leigh Hill. During the war Miss Palmer would whisper to her, 'I've got an onion if you would like one, Mrs Tyler,' because we took her our potato peelings for her chickens, so we were favoured customers.

The milkman delivered, of course, as did the baker and the coalman, but always to the back door; no tradesmen came to the front door. Where there were long terraces, the milkman would deliver to the first few houses, then would have to go back to his cart to collect more milk.

John Tyler

Pre-War House Building

One of my first jobs when I left school in 1935, aged fifteen, was with Mr Hook, a Somerset man who was building an estate of houses – which he named the Somerset estate. I earned 10s a week as the office boy in a bungalow on the corner of Somerset Avenue and Bridgewater Drive. After a year I got half-a-crown rise. Mr Hook was a former rag-and-bone man but he built good houses, and the parade of shops at Bridgewater Drive. His father was a former policeman who used to go round the site and report back to his son anybody that seemed to be slacking.

However, the building trade stopped during the war and the staff were all laid off.

Geoffrey Williams

On the Cockle Boats

I left school aged fourteen and went to work for Mr Hopkins, a corn chandler on the London Road, opposite Canvey Road. As the errand boy I earned 9s (10s but I paid 1s tax) a week, and went all over Leigh on my bike, delivering animal food.

Unloading the cockle boats, 1930s.

Then I got fed up with that and went to work on the cockle boats for more money: £5 a week – I thought I was a millionaire! We went out with the tide at all times of night and day – it wasn't worth going to bed once you'd been out and come back. We went out to the flats off Southend, Shoebury or sometimes Shellhaven, where we scraped for cockles when the tide was going out –starting as soon as the tide was above our knees, working under the water. You had high boots right up to your hips and a little net with a handle, which you leant against your leg. Then you raked the sand until the cockles came to the top and you'd rake them into your net. You'd give them a little rinse and fill up your two baskets. Then you had a pair of yokes like a dairymaid – and they were heavy! Hook them on, empty them in the boat, then start again. Heavy job that was: back-breaking work, twelve hours a day, five days a week. About eight of us were on the boat. I worked for Harvey's, then I worked for Dench.

Unloading the cockles, someone would be in the hold filling the baskets and you had to pick them up and walk down a narrow plank with a huge yoke of cockles round your neck. The plank bounced up and down and you had to bounce with it. Once you'd done it a few times it was all right: you danced with it. Then you'd empty them in the shed and go back for more. They'd cook 'em, shake 'em, put them in water and bag them up.

Sometimes on a Saturday we'd take them to sell to a cockle shop at the top of Pier Hill, but most were sent to London on the train. At the weekend they'd sell them from the huts.

Harry Bayford

Cockleshell Crush

Having been unsuccessful at gaining employment at Johnson & Jago, I was wandering disconsolately past the cockle sheds when I came to the place which now houses the Old Leigh

Museum, but which was then home to Meddle's cockle-crushing machine. There was a lad standing outside, thin and tall and maybe a year or two older than me. 'Got a light, mate?' he asked.

I carried a box of matches for just such an occasion. I didn't actually smoke myself but quite liked the idea of being thought old enough to do so, so happily obliged. We chatted for a while and the upshot was that I found myself starting work the next day with my new friend and a cheerful little old fellow who was in charge of the shed, and who told me he was seventy years old and 'still able to' – I had not the faintest idea what he was talking about.

The cockle-crusher was a large machine driven, apparently, by a belt, which vanished into a loft above it. If anything went wrong with it, the little chap would climb up a ladder, vanish through a hatch and hurl imprecations at the dratted thing whilst apparently hitting it with a large heavy instrument. It was our job, me and the other lad, to shovel huge quantities of shells into the endlessly voracious maw of this clanking contraption. Two rollers were at the bottom of the hopper and these crushed the shells into various sized pieces, which then fell onto a long sieve which vibrated backwards and forwards, falling through graduated holes onto the floor.

It was hard work keeping the hopper full of shells and, after an hour of shovelling, I found myself whinging about being a bit tired. My friend, who was shovelling shells from under the sieve into sacks being held by the old chap, offered to swap jobs and winked at me as we changed places. Two minutes later, there was an horrendous grinding crunch from the machine and it stopped dead. The old chap gave a screech of rage and leapt for the ladder with agility remarkable for his advanced years. Wisps of smoke came up from the inside of the hopper as the rollers were put into reverse and the old gent came leaping down the ladder, went crunching up the piled-up uncrushed shells and, leaning right down into the maw of the thing, emerged triumphant with a large rock.

Working at the cockle sheds. Marian Cove says, 'They'd put them in a sieve – like a big garden sieve – then they'd tip all the shells outside. People would come down and collect a bucketful to put on their gardens'. (www.FootstepsPhotos.co.uk)

He shot a baleful glance at my companion and muttered something about '****** kids wasting my ****** time!' before once again going up the ladder and setting rollers going in the right direction again. I began to realise just how fit these men were. It made me tired watching him. My friend had a pile of these rocks and large stones stashed away for use when our aching muscles felt the need.

Richard Woodley

Wartime Boat Building

My dad worked at Southend Engineering in Leigh Old Town. Naval launches used to come up; they'd whip the engine out, overhaul it and put it back in. I'd always liked boats, so I went down to Johnson & Jago and saw Len Johnson about a job.

We used to build two motor launches at a time. They'd lay the keel, stem and stern and all the frames. Then they'd winch it sideways onto the slipway and as soon as that was there, the number one gang laid another keel and what they called double diagonal planking. The worst job was riveting – the noise! Copper rivets and a layer of calico was painted in between … it was a very labour-intensive job. It was a floating time bomb – 100-octane petrol and a wooden boat.

One day, one new motor launch got jammed on the slipway. It wouldn't move. They used to melt tallow with a big blow lamp and smarm it on like thick axle grease to make it slide, but this boat got part down the slipway and we had a job to move it.

The motor launches were quite long – 112ft – and they had to launch them on a very high tide 'cos very often … well, one actually got stranded there for a few days until they got a high enough tide. There was a bloke with a steam tug, Tommy Saunt, who towed them down to Bell Wharf and moored them, then the engine was put in. On Bell Wharf there were two cranes at that time, manned by Bill Kirby, and he'd drop the engines (American engines) in from the wharf.

After the launchings, we boys got to do our favourite job out in the dinghies. You had the main cradle and hundreds of blocks of wood and we spent the afternoon, two of us in a boat, picking up all these blocks of wood – there were hundreds and hundreds of them, drifting out on the tide.

Denis Kirby

Baker, Milkman, Coalman, Dustman

In 1950 we moved to Manchester Drive. Our bread was brought every morning by Eric, the Co-op roundsman, who pulled a two-wheeled covered cart. It must have been back-breaking work and eventually he was given driving lessons and issued with an electric float, but the Howard's Dairy roundsman used a horse and cart.

When we paid the Co-op milkman, Bill, and the baker, Eric, every week a little receipt was given on which was pencilled our dividend number. I have forgotten so much in my life but not that number – 741278.

A frosty winter morning brought excitement once when the milkman's cart slid out of control when coming down Middlesex Avenue. Unable to turn left into Manchester Drive, the

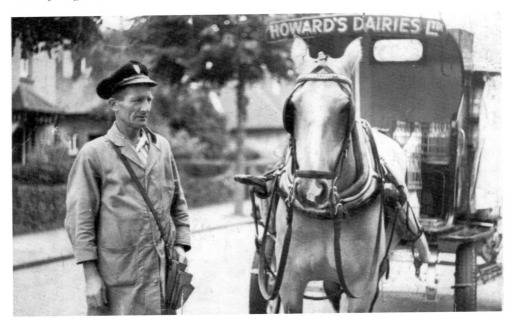

Stan Cox on his milk round, 1940s. Ruby Frost remembers, 'In the 1920s, our milkman would come round with brass churns and we would take out a jug and get it filled up.' (Keith Cox)

whole ensemble mounted the far pavement, smashed through our garden fence and came to rest by our front door. The horse was unhurt.

The coalman's lorry was a common sight: our local coal merchant was Mr Fox, whose yard was by the brook in Darlinghurst Grove.

The dustmen came once a week, as now, but then the lorry was much smaller and had sliding hatch doors, so the dustman hoisted the full bin from his shoulder, emptied the bin in the lorry, then returned the empty bin to the back garden. Our houses were terraced and rear access was by alleyways, so the dustman had two long journeys for each dustbin. Fortunately, in those still austere days there was not much rubbish to throw away. The dustbins were made of heavy steel, so you could hear the dustmen at work long before they arrived at your house.

Don Stoneman

How Much Milk?

My father, Stan Cox, was a milkman in Leigh for over thirty years. His round included the Marine Parade, where he had 'clients' rather than 'customers'. Before D-Day many soldiers were billeted on the Marine Parade and several of them were standing around outside one day when Dad came along delivering milk. A 'client' came out of her house on the corner of Thames Drive and called out to him.

'Milkman! My husband, the Colonel, is coming home for the weekend. How much milk can he have?'

'The same as a Private, Madam,' replied Dad.

The soldiers enjoyed that one!

1947 was the hardest winter in Leigh. Although only ten, I had to help my father with his milk round. The roads were so icy the horse could not pull the cart; it kept losing its footing, so Dad took it out of the shafts and tied it behind the cart and we pushed the cart.

By the late '50s, Eric Topsfield from the Co-op bakery had a petrol van and I was a milkman, working the same estate with my horse and cart. One day, I let my horse walk unaided up Middlesex Avenue, knowing he would turn into Kent Avenue and catch me up as I was delivering milk. Unfortunately, Eric had parked his van on the corner of Kent Avenue with the back doors wide open. Red Knight, my horse, decided to make a wide turn and ripped a door off Eric's van with the cart. Eric and I had to go to my parents' house in Manchester Drive and fix the door back on.

Keith Cox

Door On, Door Off

I was the manager of the VW garage and workshop in the old Empire Palace cinema building. When we moved into the building, taking it over from Pollard's Garages, we took out all the old cinema seating and the wooden flooring and transported it up to Colchester. There was a lot of grain underneath the floor, so we think the building may have been used as a grain store at one time.

There was originally only one entrance so we had a new door put in the back, for access to Oakleigh Park Drive. When the builder had finished the job, he turned his lorry round in the yard, backed into the new door and took it off again!

Ray Warman

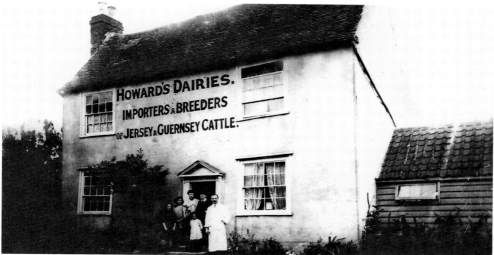

Howard's Dairies at Folly Farm. Denis Kirby says, 'The Howard's Dairies stable was at Folly Farm on the London Road with a little tiny shop where my mum used to send me in the '30s. I can remember the smell of the butter and cheese, and even the face of the lady in there.' (Roger Rolph)

Albany Laundry

My father died in 1935 and there was five of them at home, so I had to go to work. I worked in the Albany Laundry at the end of Manchester Drive so I was exempt from war service but it was hard work: the shift was from 8 a.m. to 8 p.m. When the air-raid sirens went, all the machines were turned off.

If we were on the tram and the siren went, the power went off and we'd get off and start walking. Then the power would come back on and we'd get on the tram again as it came past. Until I got a bicycle, that is, then I used to bike to the Albany. However, if the crossing gates at Leigh were shut, I had to carry my bike over the footbridge.

We moved up to North Street in 1940 when I was sixteen. When we'd had gas put in our house in the High Street, me and my brother thought it was wonderful, but at North Street we had electric and that was even better!

Renee Horner

Home for Lunch

When I first went to work in 1947, my friend Beryl and I had to walk from Rochford Corner to Priory Park and I didn't have any stockings, even in the dreadful snow that year. We still came home for lunch though, on a workman's ticket for thru'pence on the bus; we always came home because we had over an hour and you couldn't get anything to eat at work.

Winifred Stone

Working at Woolworths

My first job was in Woolworths in Leigh Broadway. I had started as a Saturday girl, and went full-time when I left school. I didn't earn much but I enjoyed it. Big tins of broken biscuits were always popular. At lunchtimes I sometimes took a sandwich and sat on St Clement's church wall to eat it. That's where we had always sat to watch the carnival go by, too.

Pat Bailey

'A Steady Old Horse'

During the 1960s, Howard's Dairies had about thirty horses stabled at their Folly Farm depot on the London Road, between Sandleigh and Fernleigh Drive. They had more horses at 251 London Road, Westcliff.

There were thirty-six milk rounds operating from Folly Farm but only three or four electric vans. There were two electric hand barrows, Graisley barrows, which you had to push a handle to operate, but they were only suitable for short local rounds.

When the Eastwood round got an electric van, I suggested that instead of getting rid of Fanny, a steady old horse, they switched her for the skittish animal that did the Chalkwell seafront round. They agreed and I got the job of taking Fanny out on her new round for the first time.

Well, from Folly Farm, Fanny was used to turning right into Darlinghurst Grove, but I wanted her to turn left into Fernleigh. She did not want to turn left! I practically had to sit on her head to get her to turn. I finally got her up to the Leigh Road where we did a few deliveries. We then went down Kings Road to Chalkwell Avenue. Over at Eastwood, Fanny had been used to eating the grass by the side of the roads but there was no grass verge at Chalkwell Avenue, so Fanny starts eating the rose bushes! I hadn't been there ten minutes before some council men came along to complain. We got some rope and I tied Fanny's head to her collar so she couldn't get down to the rose bushes.

Then we set off down Chalkwell Avenue. I let the brake off to go under the bridge and, just at that moment, a train went over the top of the bridge. Fanny went berserk! She'd never heard a train before, and she galloped off. I was on the cart but nothing would stop her; she went crazy. She finally came to a stop along by the cafés on the seafront at Westcliff and I calmed her down.

After that we had to come back to the café behind Chalkwell station, who we supplied with milk. There was a small boy eating an ice cream, who came over to look at the horse. Of course, Fanny nicked his ice cream. Then I had irate parents to deal with as well.

After all of that, I was over two hours late getting back to the depot. I told them, 'If I ever have any more bright ideas, don't take any notice of me!'

Keith Cox

Stan Cox on his milk round in the early 1960s. Keith Cox says, 'Dad worked with horses in Australia in his youth, so Howard's Dairies gave him all the difficult ones to deal with.' (Keith Cox)

Balloons and Flags

I started work as a teacher in September 1953. The 'baby bulge' of children conceived during the uncertain war years was reaching school age and school buildings could not cope with the extra numbers so I began my career in St Michael's Church hall, in Leigh Road, an outpost of Chalkwell Hall Infants School.

When I received my salary cheque for the first month – £20! A fortune! – I cycled home with it in my saddle bag and kept feeling the straps all the way home to make sure they were firmly done up. The first things I bought were a brown corduroy velvet skirt, a cream blouse and a yellow cardigan. What luxury: three new garments at once!

My first teaching year passed very quickly: working with small children is never dull. One playtime I noticed one of the little boys giving out suspicious-looking white balloons to his friends. They were blowing them up and having fun but I didn't think they should be doing that and took the balloons away. I asked the boy where he had got them from and he said he'd found them in a drawer beside Daddy's bed!

A few years later, I was teaching at Eastwood Infants School. A new block had recently been built for the Juniors and my classroom was the room that had once served as the whole school. They had blocked up the door through to the headmaster's house and sold that off. The big, black iron stove was still in the room although it didn't work, so I stood flowers on it.

Christine Selby with her first class at Chalkwell Infants School in 1954. The skirt she is wearing was bought out of her first ever pay packet. (Christine Selby *née* Blower)

North Street School staff, *c.* 1952. From left to right: Wendy Newby, Bob Lawrence, ?, Dave Williams, ?, ?, John Rombaut, Pauline Harding, ?, Miss Fowler, Mr King, Jack Batten, Miss Cobley, Miss Lake. (Wendy Newby)

One day, my class was making painted flags, which were taking a long time to dry. However, one flag seemed to dry quite quickly and I asked the owner, a gypsy girl, why she thought that was. 'The sun was shining like hell through the window,' she explained. Everyone was appalled at such bad language; in 1955 we'd never heard the like!

Christine Selby

School Secretary

I married in 1950 and soon afterwards became secretary at Leigh North Street School.

I shared an office with the headmaster, Mr King, and one day a small boy came in and announced that the cloakroom was flooded. Mr King asked him why he was telling me and not the caretaker. 'Mrs Newby always unblocks the drains,' came the reply. It was true: I did all sorts of things there – unblocking drains, first aid, playground duty, taking charge of stationery, helping with reading. There were about 450 children in the school and I knew them all; it was a lot of fun.

I once had to deal with a boy who'd cut his head when it got stuck in the railings, and joined in the hunt when another boy walked out of school and disappeared – he'd taken a bus to Southend. One girl was a very good runner and I would run against her from one side of the playground to the other to give her some practice.

I loved playing cricket with the boys, but once I hit the ball and it went straight through a window. I took myself to the headmaster's office and stood in front of his desk and said, 'Please Sir, I broke a window playing cricket.' Luckily, Mr King saw the funny side.

Wendy Newby

Mum's Wellington Boots

I was getting the hang of my new job in the cockleshell-crushing business when someone mentioned that we needed more shells.

'You'll need sea-boots,' I was told. I did not have any sea-boots, did not know where to buy them and, even if I had known, couldn't afford them. So, Mum lent me her slightly elevated wellingtons, which almost fitted me.

We – the other lad and two gents whom I did not know – travelled out to somewhere on or near Wallasea Island in an open-backed lorry, very early in the morning, in the dark.

The boat was a big disappointment: a large flat-bottomed pontoon towing four other non-powered pontoons. There was no cabin, just a sort of covered wheelhouse up front. It was 'choppy' on the way to the shellbank, which lies someway off Foulness Island.

I was so disorientated (seasick) that I never noticed that we'd actually arrived until someone suggested that I might like to get out and get some work done. However, even out of the boat, the world continued to move with fervent intensity matched only by the movement in my stomach and I tilted gracefully forward until my face collided with the hard mud and shells.

A kindly voice advised me that work would help my delicate condition and I found myself holding the sacks open as the others filled them, since I could do that job on my knees.

Flat-bottomed boats can get on the shellbank, fill up and get off on the day, apparently, so I've no idea why we had to stay overnight but I expect there was a jolly good reason. I heard the crew talking about the Shoebury gunnery range firing over the shellbank and they not knowing we were there for the night, and much muttering about real shells falling short on the cockleshells. It was quite cold; my feet were wet. I had not noticed that each of Mum's wellingtons had holes in them. I couldn't get them off because my feet had swollen up. No one appeared unduly perturbed by our situation, but as darkness began to descend with malignant inevitability, I had a passing thought that my mother most definitely would be.

We found a conventional-looking cockleboat almost upright on the mud, smug and apparently lifeless, so quiet was it in the gloom. Someone from our crew hailed the boat and within minutes we were being welcomed on board and down into the small, snug cabin. I was given some tea and must've eaten, although I don't remember what. Next, I woke up and it was morning.

On that return journey it was even choppier than the outward trip. On arrival at wherever we started out from we had to unload the sacks of shells by walking along a plank to the shore. I can't remember how I got ashore, only that my mother was there. Once home, Mum cut off the wellingtons and we stared at my corrugated feet which resembled tripe but looked worse than they felt.

My mother went and collected my pay and cards and I got another job.

Richard Woodley

Six

THE WAR YEARS AND BEYOND

War is Declared

The Second World War started when we were still on our summer holidays in September 1939. I was sitting in the garden knitting a green cardigan for schoolwear when the announcement from Neville Chamberlain in Downing Street was made over the wireless to that effect.

Everyone set about sticking up their windows with strips of brown paper, criss-crossed to guard against the effects of blast, and we were all advised to keep a wet blanket handy to put over the fireplace as a possible defence against a gas attack. Black-out curtains had to be made and strictly used as soon as it got dark or we'd be in trouble from the ARP warden. It was suggested that on hearing the wail of the siren heralding the air raid, we should shelter either under the stairs or under a table – real Dad's Army stuff – and I remember thinking my friend Jessie was very brave as she came round that same day war was declared, risking (as I thought) her life and limb to come through the streets!

The next thing that happened was that we had a letter from the school (I was then at the Southend Municipal College) telling us not to return until further notice, so we had a few glorious extra weeks holiday that year. When we did go back, we had to work through the morning until about 2.30 p.m. and then go home with satchels full of extra homework, as the dark evenings were approaching and they didn't want us to be caught in an air raid.

We had compulsorily to carry our gas masks in cardboard boxes in a string round our necks wherever we went. Later on, a few of the more individualistic types amongst us began to cover these boxes in material and use them as a kind of fashion accessory.

We were advised always to make sure the boxes contained an item of food in them as well as the gas mask, in case we were caught for a long period in a raid. Dutifully I put a bar of Aero chocolate in mine and some weeks later we actually heard a siren blowing just as we were about to go home for the afternoon. Down under the hockey pitch we went and as I sat down, my first thought was 'at last I can eat my Aero'. Alas, all my sacrifice had been in vain as when I opened the box in eager anticipation, the Aero was completely mouldy!

Phyllis Jackson

Leigh people prepare for the First World War.

Gunner to Major

By the summer of 1939 I was a gunner in the Territorial Army coast regiment which had the duty in time of war of defending the Thames and Medway from sea attacks. On 24 August I had been out with some friends to the Ritz cinema in Southend and returned home about 10.30 p.m. to be told there had been two soldiers and a policeman looking for me. On the doormat lay a blue calling-up notice that had been delivered by hand, requiring me to report forthwith to the drill hall in York Road, Southend.

I quickly changed into my uniform and my father drove me there. Later that night, I was whisked across the estuary by fast motor launch from Southend pier to the Isle of Grain where we manned a huge fort hidden in the hillside and equipped with two nine-point-two inch guns that could fire a shell weighing 380lb a distance of ten miles. War was declared ten days later and thus began six years and ten months of army service that was to take me to many locations in Britain and eventually to India, and would see me rise in rank from gunner to major.

For the first few weeks of the war, I found the transition to army life difficult and I was homesick. Then I learned how to use the range finders that enabled the guns to elevate to the exact angle required to hit their target. They had powerful telescopes and when I was not on watch, I could swing one of them round to look at Southend pier, Westcliff esplanade and Chalkwell beach. On one or two occasions I saw bounding along the beach a large black dog which I recognised as our retriever, Jock, and although it was not possible to identify individuals amongst the crowd, I knew that my father must be out for a walk along the front.

During the early months of the war little happened to change the appearance of the seafront. Then, following the German attack on France and the Low Countries, everything changed overnight. From Grain Fort, I saw strings of boats and small ships going down the estuary. A few days later some, including a destroyer, returned laden with khaki-clad men from Dunkirk. The destroyer had so many men on its deck that it rolled from side to side until I thought it would capsize but, miraculously, it stayed afloat and entered the river Medway to land the troops at Sheerness or Chatham before re-emerging and going back for another load.

Subsequently, when I went again on leave, the beach from Shoebury to Leigh had been closed off with barbed wire barricades, contractors were feverishly constructing tank traps with massive concrete blocks all along the promenade, and Nissen huts were being erected at Chalkwell on the strip of land between the beach and the road to accommodate troops and naval personnel.

Geoffrey Brown

Rampant Hedges

Immediately following Dunkirk, the local schools were evacuated. About a week later, notices appeared on lamp posts advising the residents to leave the borough voluntarily with the warning that if they remained they risked being suddenly evacuated with just one suitcase to an unspecified destination. This, of course, had the effect that those who could, left as soon as possible. I never heard of an actual compulsory evacuation taking place, although once away, one needed permission to visit the town. Our furniture went into storage and my family went to my great-aunt's in Winchmore Hill.

The dispersal was widespread, sometimes for several years – many never came back. The town became a dead one. It was astonishing how quickly it returned to nature – grass grew up through the paving stones, hedges went rampant and gardens disappeared in undergrowth.

Where people had not been able to remove their possessions before leaving, their houses presented a bleak appearance with corrugated iron placed over the doors and ground-floor windows. A house my parents owned had been slightly damaged by a landmine so we were allowed to return occasionally to it, armed with a letter of permission. We would be stopped at a 'frontier' at Rawreth where the police or soldiers would enter the coach and examine our identity cards and our letter before we were allowed to proceed! As the fear of invasion diminished, people drifted back and in 1943 we returned to Leigh.

Norman Crane

Wartime Childhood

During the war I played in the fields between Leigh station and Hadleigh, making dens and watching the dog fights overhead. Many's the time we were down there during the Battle of Britain – we didn't appreciate that there was any danger. There were three ponds, which we called number one, two and three, where we took our fishing nets to catch sticklebacks. Other times, we'd take a box of matches, light a little fire and bake potatoes up at Hadleigh Castle for our lunch.

Bombed houses at Manchester Drive. Ruby Frost says, 'Everyone was so friendly during the war; everyone talked to everyone else.' (Reg Sims)

My friend, Alan Stivey, and I once scrumped some apples from the back gardens of the bomb -damaged houses in Westleigh Avenue and took them down to eat in the fields by Leigh station, together with a pack of woodbines that Alan had 'acquired' from his father's newsagent's at the top of Belton Way. We were only aged eight or nine and were as sick as dogs and never smoked again.

After air raids, we'd get on our bikes and go off around the roads to see if we could find any shrapnel. Up at Belfairs there were artillery firing at the aircraft and we'd go round there in the mornings looking for shrapnel – horrible pieces of metal; we didn't appreciate how lethal they could be. I always kept an eye out for it while I did my paper round.

At home we had an Anderson shelter where, as far as we children were concerned, it was fun to sleep in the summer months whether there was an air raid or not.

We always had a roast joint on the Sunday, then cold meat on Monday, mince on Tuesday and, if there was anything left, stew on Wednesday. I never liked stew, so I went up to the Civic Restaurant in St Clement's Church hall.

For part of the war, some flats at the bottom of Leighville Grove were occupied by soldiers – Scottish regiments. We liked to ask them if they had any spare badges to collect and they'd usually give us some. There were plenty of soldiers about just before D-Day.

David Flack

'You'll Be Killed!'

I was at Westcliff High School when we received the order to evacuate and I was concerned that there wouldn't be any education available in Southend, so I chose to go to Chapel-en-le-Frith with the school. I was away for fourteen months, during which I was most unhappy. Then I took my matriculation and decided I was going home because I was so homesick: I'd had enough. So, I came home and I started work in the Midland Bank in London.

However, at home, the police came round to every house and told everyone they had to get out. There was absolute panic, and my parents quickly found a house at Buckhurst Hill.

We visited Leigh once or twice during the war and found it to be deserted. Grass, flowers and other vegetation was growing between the pavement flagstones; the road was like a field and fruit lay rotting on the ground because there was nobody around to collect it; it was such a shame.

I remember 1940 as a beautiful summer, despite the dog fights overhead. Mother and I were standing watching one on our way home from Hadleigh once, when Mr Stibbards ran out from the undertaker's and cried, 'Don't stand there looking at those! You'll be killed!' and he took us in until the fight was over.

Sylva Sheffield

No School

Eastwood School closed down in the war, so I just stayed at home. My mother went to work at the Albany Laundry and I was left on my own. I used to stand outside and watch the dog fights overhead.

I remember the doodlebugs: one dropped in Park Avenue and blew several houses to pieces; a girl I knew got buried beneath it and several of her neighbours were also killed. I also remember the V1 that dropped near Eastwood School at Christmas time. If we'd been in school we would have had it. At least you got the siren when the doodlebugs were coming and you could hear them. With the V1s you didn't get anything; they just came out of the blue.

Bombed houses at Pavilion Drive. Mike Grimwade remembers, 'The foundations of the bombed houses were our playground.' (Reg Sims)

After Dunkirk they brought soldiers back to the Drill Hall in Eastwood Road North and put them in the houses. 'Bellevue' on the Rayleigh Road was full of spitfire pilots and Mum used to work for them, washing their football kits, while I used to try and darn their socks. Actually, pilots were all over the place. Some who were living in 'the Mount' kept chickens in the house.

Winifred Stone

'Your French Doors Are Open!'

So many people left the area that there were only two families left in Madeira Avenue during the war. In 1942 I passed the scholarship exam and joined the boys from Westcliff High School in Belper, Derbyshire. However, I was only there a few months before we came back home, just in time for the bombing of Manchester Drive, not far from our home. Having said that, the bombing did not wake my family at all and the first we knew of it was our next-door neighbour shouting: 'Mr Tyler! Mr Tyler! Your French doors have blown open!'

Another neighbour bred King Charles spaniels. When there was an air raid, she would get up, put the dogs in the Morrison shelter and then go back to bed.

The National Savings Group secretaries had to report to my father, who was head of the Leigh scheme. When I was twelve, I was in charge of the stationery and at thirteen I was the Group

The 'Leigh Commandos', c. 1947. John Tyler explains, 'I am in the centre my mother, Liz Bowthorbe and with other National Savings Street Group secretaries in Blenheim Crescent. We were knocking on every door to see if we could find somebody to take on the job of Street Group secretary.' (John Tyler)

National Savings fund-raising shop in Leigh
Broadway, opposite St Clement's church, 1944.
John Tyler, Mrs Percival, Mrs De Vere, Mrs Tyler,
Mrs Pratt and Mr Tyler. (John Tyler)

Secretary for Scarborough Drive. I had an oxo tin for my change and stock of saving stamps, and I would go round and sell stamps to the residents for sixpence, a shilling, or 2s 6d.

Once a year, during National Savings Week, we took a shop and sold as many stamps and savings certificates as we could. When it was Spitfire Week, we raised £20,000 in one week in Leigh. After the schools came back from evacuation and the town began to pick up again, there were still loads of empty houses but we tried to have a National Savings Group in every street in Leigh.

Shortly before D-Day, most of the empty houses were commandeered by the army; soldiers were brought into the town and billeted in them. We had English soldiers in Madeira Avenue but I believe Woodfield Avenue had Czech soldiers.

A doodlebug once cut out right over our house and then cruised down to crash at the corner of Oakwood Avenue and the Arterial Road. We could see the plume of smoke go up and my brother leapt on his bike and went to see what had happened. Another time, over 2,000 homes were damaged when they dropped landmines on Vardon Drive and Westleigh Avenue.

They once dropped sticks of incendiary bombs on my neighbourhood but every one fell in the middle of the road – they melted the tarmac in the road but very luckily missed the houses. However, high-explosive bombs destroyed houses in both Dawlish Drive and Leigh Hall Road.

Although the air raids at night were very frightening, bombed-out houses were nothing special to us, and we didn't take much notice of them as we walked by on our way to school.

John Tyler

Freezing Cold

Towards the end of the war, when I was a small boy, I lived with my grandmother in the flat above 2 Rectory Grove. In fact, every room was filled with different sections of the family who had fled London for the relative safety of Leigh. However, there was no fuel afforded or available for heating; there was no coal in the place at all, so no fires in the grates. Instead of the Blitz, the family faced considerable squalor and overcrowding as there were too many people living there for the size of the place. It was freezing cold and damp and birds got in through holes in the roof.

Michael Young

Mr and Mrs Tyler at the National Savings shop, Broadway West, 1945. John Tyler says, 'During the war, my father would take over an empty shop for a week and we'd sell as many savings certificates as we could in that week.'

Torch in a Tin

There were plenty of soldiers in the empty houses in Leigh during the war – you just accepted it. There was no trouble but there was always soldiers around.

Skateboards were popular with us youngsters; I'd get a skate and put a board on it, then sit down on the board and go down the road. Also, we'd get an old bicycle tyre around our waists and use it like a hula hoop.

There were no lights allowed during the black-out, of course, and one foggy day I was coming home from Southend and called round to see a friend of mine who lived near Chalkwell School. When I came out, I thought, 'This is the right way,' but I ended up back in Southend! And I'd only had a few yards to go down to our road!

However, you were supposed to have lights on your bike, so we had a torch with a big front on it, with a double battery in it. Then we'd get an old condensed milk tin, take the top off, cutting a slit in it, and put it in the torch, behind the glass; just a slit of light would show. By the way, the condensed milk had been eaten on bread.

Harry Bayford

Evacuation

On Sunday 2 June 1940, two days after my sixteenth birthday I left our front gate at four or five o'clock in the morning and walked to Westcliff High School carrying my gas mask and case.

From there we were driven off, not knowing where we were going or when we would see our parents again. We eventually arrived at Belper in Derbyshire on what was the hottest day of the year; the tar was melting in the road. Then the local people came and took us in ones and twos. I was one of the last four left and a lady came and took pity on us. Her husband had said, 'Don't you dare come back with an evacuee!' so she took two of us!

I was in Derbyshire for thirteen months, during which there were many air raids, when we would get into the Morrison shelter under the table in the living room. If the siren went after 9 p.m. and the all clear didn't sound until midnight, we were allowed to have the following morning off school.

Back in Leigh, our house in Marine Avenue was damaged when a landmine fell in Westleigh Avenue and my family had to move out. They decided to go to Hackney and arrived just in time for the Blitz! During raids, my father had to stay at work while my mother and sister spent quite a few nights down in the underground station.

Derek Rowe

Ack-Ack Guns

I remember sitting on a coach outside St Hilda's school waiting for evacuation when someone announced that we weren't going to have a war after all, and we all got off the coach – we were ever so disappointed. To make up for it, they took us to Whipsnade Zoo instead, where an elephant ate one of the girls' panama hats.

However, there *was* a war and we were evacuated to a great big house in Somerset but got in trouble for climbing over the roof.

Mother and Father had to get out of our house at Salisbury Road because the army took over the whole road. However, our house, No. 19, stood empty – although there were soldiers next-door. They pulled down all the banisters there for the fire, to keep warm. Worse, we found when we came back from evacuation that somebody had pinched my doll's pram out of the garage – I was furious about that!

We used to walk over to Belfairs and the Old Vienna for a cup of tea. During the war, there were huge ack-ack guns all along the drive up to the house, with buildings housing the facilities for the people manning the guns. They say that more tiles were taken off the roofs of Leigh from those guns than by enemy bombs – they didn't half go off with a crack!

Betty Smith

Everyone Disappeared

During the war everyone disappeared from Leigh and there were roads and roads of empty houses. My family evacuated to Dorking, where I made friends with a German Jewish girl whose family had sent her over from Germany. One wet night, we went out when this plane appeared from nowhere and machine gunned all down Dorking High Street. We got down behind a wall and crouched down under our umbrella, hearing bullets bouncing all around us.

Towards the end of the war we moved back to Bailey Road and I became a dressmaker and then went into tailoring. My cousins had a tailor's in Rectory Grove. I worked on a lot of alterations because people couldn't afford to buy new. And, of course, we were short of materials during the war and for some time afterwards.

Joan Herbert

ARP Warden

I worked at the Albany Laundry during the war and I was also an air-raid warden, based at the ARP post by the Ship pub. The night shift was 10 p.m. to 6 a.m. when we had to patrol round in pairs and make sure no one was showing a light, and see if there were any incendiary bombs. We slept at the wardens' posts and after the night shift, my mum had to come to wake me up. There was another ARP post in the library gardens, down a manhole, but I said there was no way I was sleeping down there! Later, I was moved up to an ARP post in The Broadway on the corner of Victoria Road.

There were a lot of soldiers about who had come down for a month's training and were billeted in some of the houses left by people who had moved away. I used to walk down Church Hill at 10 p.m. and there would be lots of soldiers walking about, but I never felt afraid of them.

Although many people moved away, Leigh was never completely evacuated. Down in the High Street and The Broadway, all the shops stayed open the same as usual all through the war.

My husband went to Dunkirk on the *Letitia*, owned by Mr Dench. His boat was towing the *Renown*, and the *Renown* blew up. When he came back he went back on the barges for a few months, then joined up with the navy and went on the minesweepers.

After the soldiers had been here about a month, all the army lorries were lined up along the Marine Parade, ready to go. We didn't know where they were going then but later found out it was D-Day.

Renee Horner

Commuting to Baddow

In 1940, I volunteered for the WAAF but my eyesight let me down in the medical and, instead, I got a job at Marconi's at Chelmsford, keeping records of employees.

To get to Chelmsford from Leigh, I took the bus from the Grand Hotel at 6.30 a.m. to Victoria Circus. From there I took a train to Shenfield, where I changed for a train to Chelmsford. Later, I transferred to Baddow research laboratories. Then I had to make the same journey plus getting another bus from Chelmsford to Baddow. At Baddow I had to wait for a bus which only ran once an hour to Southend and if it was full I had to wait for the next one. If a car drew up and offered you a lift, you got in. It was only people with essential jobs who got petrol, so you knew you'd be all right.

Sometimes I could cycle to Southbourne Grove and get a lift to work with someone who had a petrol ration. He had a Morris Minor with a windscreen that opened and headlamps with louvres on so that only little slits of light could be seen in the black-out. One foggy evening we were peering out of it all the way home; that was a nightmare. I hated the black-out – you had to stand for a long time to get used to the dark if you came out of a lighted place.

My dad was in charge of an air-raid warden post just off The Broadway in Victoria Road. We were all supposed to help and, therefore, aged twenty-one, I trained as a warden too. In first aid training we learned all about gases and were taught how to deliver a baby! Luckily, I never had to put that into use! If you were on the rota to man the warden's post you were in charge of the telephone all night. There were two fold-up canvas camp beds, so you could lie down, but if anything came through on the phone, you just locked up and went. I was on duty when there was a bomb dropped on Westleigh Avenue, so I had to go up there on my bike to see if I could be useful or take messages. I remember my brother was about and they needed a car moved and my brother, then aged about fifteen, said 'I can do it', and he did.

Very often I'd be up all night carrying out duties, fire watching, etc,. but I still had to get the bus at 6.30 a.m. every morning to get to work in Chelmsford. Often I didn't even have time to change out of my uniform and would arrive at work in my warden's uniform. But we didn't think anything of it then; we just took it all in our stride.

Ruby Frost

Open House for Soldiers

The schools returned from evacuation in 1942 (when the war was really getting hot!) to find Leigh practically empty of residents.

All the women had to take a job unless they had children under five years old, so my mother found herself a job quick, working on Wellington bombers at E.K. Cole, before she could be allocated to a munitions factory. Her job entailed working out the amount of wiring needed for the Wellington bomber panels from drawings.

We lived on the corner of Henry Drive. Soldiers were billeted in houses all around us and army lorries were parked nose to tail along the roads. Across the road, No. 35 Walker Drive served as the army's Officers' Mess.

There were Canadian Scots soldiers in Highlands Boulevard, all dressed up in their regalia. They'd whistle and shout whenever I walked by, which made me cringe.

However, Mum kept an open house for everyone and soldiers were always round. Mum, a widow, was friendly with Mr Dodds, the man in charge of Rochford airport fighter station, so we had plenty of the air force in our house too, even the Australian Air Force. Any time of the day or night, they knew they'd be welcome and sometimes they'd land and come straight over from the airport still in their flying boots.

At night, Mum and I would lie in bed with the curtains open and watch the war going on: the searchlights, flashes of guns and bombs going off. Some of the ack-ack guns from Belfairs were pulled through the streets on the back of lorries, following the aircraft – and then we really would hear them crash!

We knew something was up in the run-up to D-Day. I watched the young soldiers smear yellow gunge all around the wheels of the trucks and lorries, which I now realise was to make them water-tight for the beach landings. Of course, they had to leave with just what they stood up in, so they brought us all sorts of things they couldn't take with them: bedding and tins of food, and we were very grateful.

Mother was out the night before they left and I was sitting doing my homework. There was a knock at the door and a very young officer, aged nineteen or twenty, was standing there with a bottle of scotch in his hand. He wanted me to go up to Hadleigh Castle with him but I said I couldn't because I had to get on with my homework; I was only fourteen. He didn't want to leave and I could see that he was frightened to death because he knew what was coming, but eventually I persuaded him to go. The next day the place was deserted – everybody had gone; all the lorries gone from the roads and the soldiers gone from the houses. I never saw that young officer again.

I also remember the ships and landing barges lined up along the Thames, ready for the invasion. Then the weather closed down: it rained. The ships were so closely packed it was lucky the Germans didn't come over or they'd have been finished. Then suddenly they were gone.

Ellen King

Young Mother at Home

During the war we were living in Cambridge but we'd get a permit once a month to visit my in-laws and to collect vegetables from my parents' garden and allotment in Leigh. The place was almost deserted with no traffic, no birds and very few people. Grass was growing down the middle of Hadleigh Road and street after street was deserted except where soldiers were billeted.

Soldiers were next door to Mother and Dad, who let them come in to use their bath and Mother did mending for them.

Dad was Chief Air Raid Warden and had to go out on duty during raids. Mother also went out fire watching but gave it up when I moved down, so she could be with the baby and me. We used to get the bombers and doodlebugs going over on their way to London and, of course, the ack-ack fire with shrapnel falling into the streets. It was a very worrying time.

Joy Perkins

Church Parade in Kilts

I was evacuated with St Bernard's to New Mills, Derbyshire. When we came back to Leigh there were soldiers everywhere. They practised with their bayonets on the grass opposite our house on Marine Parade, with straw sacks hanging up and blood-curdling screams as they ran towards them.

We had the 51st Highland Division billeted in Hamboro Gardens, who would march along the Marine Parade with their pipes and kilts to church parade at St Clement's every Sunday.

As D-Day approached, we knew something was going on because the estuary was chock-a-block full of boats. I hung out of my bedroom window when the planes and gliders started coming over and counted over 300 before I gave up – the sky was full of them!

I didn't join the celebrations on VE Day or VJ Day as I was on duty as a children's nurse for both of them – just my luck to miss all the celebrations!

Shirley Rowe

Evacuation and Starting Work

After Dunkirk, Westcliff High School was given one week's notice to evacuate to Belper in Derbyshire, while the children at North Street went to New Mills. It was a lot of excitement for me as a fourteen-year-old. We arrived at school at 5 a.m. one Sunday morning with one suitcase carrying our essentials – I've still got my suitcase! I was wearing a cap, grey jacket, shorts and long socks, and carried a satchel and a gas mask on a strap. We were taken to Southend Central station where there was a notice up saying, 'No passenger services today'.

A long train stood at each of the six platforms, waiting to take children away. The older masters, those not called up, went with us and were effectively on duty twenty-four hours a day for the two years we were away.

Later, my parents were away when a bomb dropped in Westleigh Avenue and they received a telegram from a neighbour warning that we no longer had a front door. When we got home, we had to have new doors and windows. In fact, during the war only three houses in Burnham Road were family-occupied; the others were occupied by troops. My mother worked for the WRVS at a canteen at the Leigh Wesley Church.

The trams disappeared from Leigh in Easter 1941 when the rails were taken for the war effort, as were the railings from around Marine Gardens. Before the war you had to use a stile at the end of Rectory Grove to get in.

I returned from evacuation in July 1942 and worked for Mr Verinder in Rectory Grove selling stationery until I was offered a job at the Bank of England. The bank was full of old men brought back from retirement but they were not allowed a morning break as they were so busy. I was called up three days after my eighteenth birthday and one week later I was in the army.

VE Day was not very happy for us because I only had a couple of days' embarkation leave before being sent off to fight the Japanese. However, I returned to Leigh in November 1947 and by then the town had begun to brighten up.

Donald Fraser

Ghost Town

During the war, Leigh became a ghost town. Most non-essential people had left voluntarily. One had to receive special permission to enter the locality and this we did in order to visit our parents. A waste plot adjoining Joy's dad's garage at 101 Hadleigh Road became a source of food and we loaded up the car with as much produce as we could carry back to our home in Cambridge. We also took back two black cat refugees, whose family had moved out.

I was stationed in Verona when news of the German surrender came through. I was instructed to report to Catterick and immediately began my journey home. I phoned home with the news that I was catching the next train to Leigh. I raced up Belton Way, turned the corner into Hadleigh Road and there was my little daughter running towards me as fast as her little legs could carry her. It was a great joy; one of those precious moments of my life.

Arthur Perkins

VE Day (may be VJ Day) in Croft Close. (Don Stoneman)

VE Day celebrations in North Street. Pat Bailey, just right of centre, is being held by her father, who she had only recently met. (Pat Bailey *née* Humphress)

Signed Over the Bar

I was six when war was declared. We moved to Bristol but after one particular air raid in which bombs were dropped along our road, Dad packed us into the car and we drove off into Wales.

We moved back to Leigh when the doodlebugs were still arriving. Apparently, someone had taken Dad's small boat over to Dunkirk, ferrying soldiers to the bigger boats and making several trips back to England but, sadly, his boat was stolen soon afterwards. Dad was able to catch up with his friends down in Old Leigh and was in the Peterboat when peace was announced and they all signed their names over the bar.

Doris Williams

The children on North Street on VE Day (may be VJ Day). Pat Bailey is centre front, holding the hand of her cousin David. (Pat Bailey)

'The War is Over!'

The first I knew about VE Day was when someone knocked on our door and said, 'The war is over!' We pulled our curtains open and put all the lights on in the house. Then we opened the front door and went out with saucepan lids and sticks and made a great deal of noise, dancing around in Henry Drive and Walker Drive. We shouted and we sang.

Ellen King

Victory Peal

I began to learn church bell ringing about 1944, aged sixteen. During those war years, of course, bell ringing was banned, so the bells were tied and did not make a noise. Frank Lufkin, the verger of St Mary's, Prittlewell was my ringing teacher. He became a fireman during the war and ringing practice had to fit in with his fireman's duties.

There were no very experienced bell ringers at St Clement's during the war, so Frank found himself in charge of organising the ringing of peals to celebrate VE Day. It was not an easy job with the shortage of ringers. Although I had only been ringing for a year or so, I was asked to join the peal at Leigh on Friday 11 May 1945.

Three ringers were boys not long returned from the Midlands: Frank Howard, who was at Westcliff High School, on treble, me on the second, and another Southend High School boy, Richard Dixon, on third. As we'd learnt to ring when the bar on ringing was still in force, we'd never had a chance to hear our bells. William Perry on fourth was quite elderly and had spent his life as a bricklayer. I remember him as a stout, white-haired and jolly little fellow. Frank Lufkin was on fifth and conducted the band. Charles Chambers ringing the tenor was another elderly man who drummed very well and kept the band moving along. We went straight into the peal and rang for two hours and forty-five minutes continuously.

Bernard Sadler

Turned up at School

VE Day was announced late at night — midnight, I think — and we were told that it would be a school holiday. We weren't quite sure if they meant the next day because of the time of the announcement, so we all turned up at school and were told we could go home again.

There were street parties in Manchester Drive, Kent Avenue and Norfolk Avenue, but it was difficult with the rationing.

John Tyler

VE Day in Leighville Grove, looking north. David Flack says, 'We had a main table down the middle of the road and additional tables on the path. We're all there in the photos: the Yetts, the Allens, the Flacks, the Warners, the Cotgroves – everybody in the road knew each other'. (David Flack)

VE Day, Leighville Grove, looking south. (David Flack)

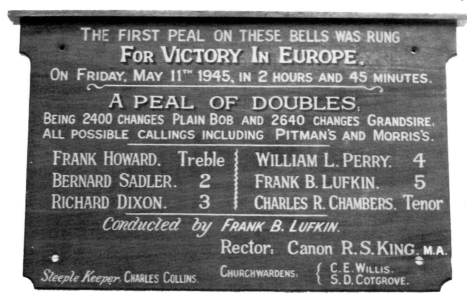

THE FIRST PEAL ON THESE BELLS WAS RUNG
FOR VICTORY IN EUROPE.
ON FRIDAY, MAY 11ᵀᴴ 1945, IN 2 HOURS AND 45 MINUTES.

A PEAL OF DOUBLES,
BEING 2400 CHANGES PLAIN BOB AND 2640 CHANGES GRANDSIRE.
ALL POSSIBLE CALLINGS INCLUDING PITMAN'S AND MORRIS'S.

FRANK HOWARD. Treble   WILLIAM L. PERRY. 4
BERNARD SADLER. 2   FRANK B. LUFKIN. 5
RICHARD DIXON. 3   CHARLES R. CHAMBERS. Tenor

Conducted by FRANK B. LUFKIN.

Rector: Canon R. S. KING. M.A.

Steeple Keeper: CHARLES COLLINS.   CHURCHWARDENS: { C. E. WILLIS. / S. D. COTGROVE.

Plaque commemorating the first peal of St Clement's bells, rung for Victory in Europe, 11 May 1945.

Singing in the Road

Come VE Day, my husband was still away with the navy, fighting the Japanese from HMS *Sussex*. I thought, 'It's all right for people whose men are safe!' Bank staff like me had to go into work on VE Day but, as a matter of fact, it was quite fun because the girls I worked with in London all walked down to St Paul's where a service was going on. Then we all linked arms and walked back down Cheapside, singing in the middle of the road. Later, back home, my sister and I walked along the front to Westcliff and joined in the dancing at the bandstand.

Sylva Sheffield

House Hunting

In the summer of 1945, my wife and I came on leave and contemplated buying a house in Leigh. Many houses were still unoccupied, having been vacated hurriedly in 1940, and quite a lot were for sale. Walking round the roads in Leigh, one saw the ravages caused by five years of neglect. None of the houses had been painted; some had lost tiles or windows and there were some cracks in walls. Fences had fallen down, gardens were overgrown, grass grew high and straggly, with roses or brambles spilling over the front walls obstructing pavements with long, barbed tendrils. Dust and dirt lay on window ledges, mildew and rot pervaded interiors and woodworm thrived. Parts of the town, particularly near the seafront, had become desolate, derelict areas.

Prices doubled in the twelve months following May 1945, and those who were lucky enough to buy a house began the long and difficult task of paying for it and restoring it.

VJ Day celebrations in Leighville Grove. (David Flack)

Along the seafront, it did not take long to remove the barbed wire and open the beach to leisure use. The concrete tank traps took a bit longer to demolish but gradually the evidence of wartime disappeared. Hotels and boarding houses took down their shutters and reopen for business. Ice creams and bananas were again on sale and Chalkwell beach resumed the aura of holiday-making.

However, the beach did not go back completely to the halcyon days of the 1930s. The minstrels had gone for ever; the newsvendor never returned to his pitch on the promenade; the boating pool by the Crowstone gradually silted up and the little boats were not brought back. Otherwise, the town revived as a holiday resort.

Geoffrey Brown

Cycling in the Snow

In the 1947 snows I had to cycle from Salisbury Road to Bournemouth Park Road where I was a teacher. I remember my bike sliding from under me on the Leigh Road. Later, Dad lent me his motorbike for the journey.

When they were building St Aidan's they began by removing the turf and I went down there with my big pram and got some for our garden. The Belfairs housing estate shot up very quickly and it was a right mess while they were getting the water and everything laid on.

I enjoyed ballroom dancing in the upstairs hall in Leigh police station, where you paid for a season ticket for lessons.

Betty Smith

Back to the Office

In the terrible cold winter of 1947, I returned to my job at the Midland Bank. I remember the snow well: burst pipes, water running down the stairs, Dad up in the loft. Leigh station was like a parade ground because a lot of us wore our wartime greatcoats and flying jackets: it was full of ex-army, navy and air force types all going back to the city. I went up to town once in my flying boots because it was so cold. On the Belfairs estate, the milkman's horse couldn't get up the hill at Thorndon Park Close in the snow.

Derek Rowe

Highlands Methodist Church Social Club

I joined the Highlands Club in 1948 and became the secretary with Audrey Losa. The club choir went out several times a year to give concerts to OAP clubs and had a combined show once a year with the drama group. We used the old church, now the hall, so there was a lot of preparation and clearing up involved, ready for church services. We joined the church choir when the new building was opened, leading the procession into the church when it was officially opened in July 1956.

Joy Perkins

A Borrowed Coat

When I moved from school to secretarial college, clothes became important. Despite still using clothing coupons, we were all decked out in dirndl skirts and white skinny-rib sweaters and jellybean hats, which we knitted. Other 'must-haves' were Tangee lipstick (a ghastly orange colour) and 'Evening in Paris' perfume (Woolworths) and we thought we were the bees' knees.

By this time I had met Fred, who lived opposite us in Grasmead Avenue. We learned ballroom dancing and went horseriding in Belfairs Woods and the common behind it. Walking along the seafront to the pier and back was a cheap way of spending an evening as we were saving hard. When Fred had a day off work one day, I sneaked my older sister Marjorie's jacket from her wardrobe and we caught the train to London to visit the Festival of Britain, viewing the Skylon, the Dome of Discovery and the Battersea Funfair. Quite a day! I managed to put Marjorie's coat back without her knowledge – until our photos were developed! Whoops!

Doris Williams

Maintaining Telephone Communication

By 1953, I was employed by the Telephone Department of the Post Office. On the morning of Sunday 1 February, my boss phoned to say he had heard on the radio that parts of Canvey Island had been flooded. He asked me to find out if the telephone system had been affected.

Highlands Methodist Church ladies' choir, 1965. (Joyce Perkins *née* Attwood)

I ran down to the Marine Parade and I was amazed to find Canvey Island had disappeared and in its place was a vast area of sea: there was nothing but water.

I was nonplussed. I could see that our staff at the manual exchange on Canvey could be in trouble. Some action had to be taken. I went to the Southend exchange and found the number of enquiry calls had swamped the automatic equipment, so I got the police to agree to tour the town with their loud-speaker van to ask people not to phone. This was to allow calls to get through from more distant places. I was able to speak to the Canvey Island exchange operators to find that they were still operating.

I decided to try and get to the Canvey exchange and take some food with me. The official car took me as near as possible: the Red Cow pub on Long Road. I managed to find a boat and we rowed along between the houses on Long Road until we came to the exchange, which was housed in a bungalow on one of the side roads. I shall never forget that journey or the look of relief on the faces of the two operators. They were standing in about 2ft of seawater. The mainframe, fortunately, was just above the watermark. I stayed there to ensure telephone communication was maintained and while I was there the water receded. The Red Cow has since changed its name to King Canute.

Arthur Perkins

Filling Sandbags

In 1953, I was serving behind the bar of the Ship when they came in and asked if there was anyone with a boat who could help. Of course, all the fishermen turned out of the bar and got in their boats to see what they could do.

The girls of the Ivy Meynell Secretarial College in Nelson Road, 24 July 1947, including: Pamela Fretten, Ethel Noakes, June Hull, Dorothy Stallard, Jean McMillan, Iris Grant, Shirley Sandford, Patricia Sampson, Joan Dance, Joyce Collins, Beryl Kerton, Marie Graham, Sheila Skelt, Juliet Cole, Ivy Maynell, Maureena McCarthy, Joan Wilkes, Pat Bradley. (Doris Williams *née* Rowley)

The next day, Leigh station was like a swimming pool and no trains were running, so I couldn't go to work. I went down to the Bay (Bell Wharf) and helped out by filling sandbags. Anyone who could help was down there doing what they could and lorries came down and took the sandbags away.

Leigh people knew all about floods because the spring tides used to flood the cottages down in the Old Town every year and people were used to carting all their furniture upstairs.

Albert Plummer

Called for Boats

I was in St Clement's Church in the middle of the service on 1 February 1953 when they came in and called for dinghies to go to Canvey. Leigh station was flooded but they laid on a bus to Benfleet. Even there, water was up to the platform. My husband and his sister went down to the cliffs and saw the railway signals sticking out of the water.

Shirley Rowe

Little Scraps of Paper

In 1953 my mother was running the office at the Essex Caravan Centre on the London Road by Sutherland Boulevard. It usually opened seven days a week, but one Sunday morning we were just sitting down to breakfast when her boss knocked on our door and said he wasn't going to open that day, he was going down to Canvey Island because it had been flooded. He was ex-army and we could see his car was loaded up with all sorts of equipment.

Somehow I found myself down at Benfleet police station, sitting upstairs at a big desk. They'd come in and dump little scraps of paper on the desk, inscribed with the names and addresses of people they'd taken off Canvey. My job was to unwrap these little balls of paper and enter the names into a register. I was there for hours.

Ellen King

An Old Gentleman

On 1 February 1953, I looked out of my bedroom window in New Road and didn't realise at first that I could only see the sea. Canvey was completely covered. Quite a lot of us went out to the wharf to see what was happening and found they were bringing refugees across from Canvey direct to Leigh. We took in an old gentleman and looked after him at home for a fortnight until his relations came from London to pick him up.

Connie Satchwell

Cows on the Sea Wall

On Saturday 31 January 1953, we were bent against the wind walking home along Rectory Grove. On the Sunday morning my parents were both unwell and I couldn't get the kettle to boil because the gas was low. My brother came round and told us the extent of the floods and the plight of the people on Canvey Island. He took his boat over to Canvey and rowed people ashore. I couldn't go as I was looking after my parents.

I saw cows walking along the top of the sea wall. People from Canvey Point were rescued by boats and brought to Bell Wharf, where ambulances waited to take them straight to hospital.

The railway at Leigh was completely under water and they bussed us to Rayleigh station to get on a train. It was a week before the water subsided at Leigh and the trains ran again.

After that, all the sea walls were raised and a bridge was built for the lorries with rubbish to cross the creek. Previously, there was no bridge to Two Tree Island and I had been able to sail right around the island in August 1939. I'm pretty sure that one of the 'two trees' had already fallen before the war.

Norman Crane

Moving to Old Leigh

I moved to Old Leigh in 1954. It was a lovely fishing village; just as you'd expect a fishing village to be. My husband was a controller on the railway and all the houses in Old Leigh belonged to the railway, so they offered us one. Everybody who lived there was kind; everybody was welcoming. Our daughters loved to go down to the beach every day or to sit on the wall at the back of the Peterboat. It was very safe for them because everyone knew everyone else in those days. As the flyover had not yet been built, the only way out was the railway crossing gate — it was a very quiet place to live.

You didn't get the crowds in Old Leigh that you get now, except on bonfire night. Then, the East Enders used to come down and we had to block the letterbox up to stop people putting fireworks through it. They built big bonfires on the beach —literally hundreds of people came down here, and maybe two policemen and a dog would be sent down to keep an eye on things. The youngsters once pushed on the crossing gates and broke them and stopped all the trains.

Irene Reynolds

Building development

In the late '50s, Brickhouse Farm was sold off and they began building along Blenheim Chase. We young lads didn't like that because it was part of *our* area. The contractors would stake out the plots and put in markers for the houses. When they came back the next day they'd find that somehow, mysteriously, overnight all their markers had disappeared … but they won in the end.

Mike Grimwade

Other titles published by The History Press

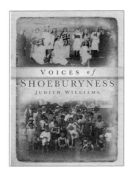

Voices of Shoeburyness
JUDITH WILLIAMS

Shoeburyness has witnessed a century of change, from the comings and goings of two world wars to its eventual absorption into its much larger neighbour, Southend. This book comprises the memories of more than fifty people who lived and worked in Shoeburyness between 1919 and 1970. Individually, these stories are interesting; together they create a fascinating picture of a Shoebury that has long gone.

978-0-7524-5223-4

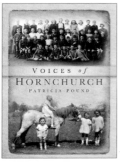

Voices of Hornchurch
PATRICIA POUND

Hornchurch was once a rural village, though it has now been swallowed up by Greater London. This nostalgic, moving and deeply personal set of recollections discusses this change – which may be seen in the archive photographs which complement the text – and reveals how the village of the past became the town of today. *Voices of Hornchurch* will delight locals and visitors alike.

978-0-7524-6036-9

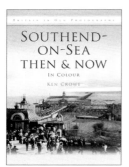

Southend-on-Sea Then & Now
KEN CROWE

Southend-on-Sea has gone through many transformations since the Middle Ages. Having acquired the name 'South End', the area changed when a 'New Town' was built along the cliffs to the west. The arrival of the railway in the mid-nineteenth century, and the subsequent influx of seaside day trippers, boosted Southend's popularity, and it quickly expanded into a large and bustling town. This fascinating photographic history explores the changes through carefully chosen snapshots.

978-0-7524-6323-0

Haunted Southend
DEE GORDON

The popular seaside resort of Southend-on-Sea has long been a haven for holidaymakers, but the town also harbours some disturbing secrets … Discover the darker side of Southend with this spooky collection of spine-chilling tales from around the town. From ghostly sightings in Hadleigh Castle, ominous sounds and smells on the seafront, and tales of mysterious shapes at the town's pubs and taverns, this book is guaranteed to make your blood run cold.

978-0-7524-6082-6

Visit our website and discover thousands of other History Press books.

www.thehistorypress.co.uk